Here are more than 45 lovely recipes that add a dash of floral decadence to snacks, treats, and other refreshments. Enjoy a Calendula, Gouda, and Bacon Quiche for brunch; Orange Blossom and Chamomile Chocolate Pumpkin Bread as an afternoon snack; or a Garden Party Layer Cake after dinner. Plus, you'll find plenty of pantry staples for adding an elegant touch to any dish. Tips for choosing, sourcing, and growing edible blooms round out this compendium of botanical delights.

FLORAL
PROVISIONS

FLORAL

PROVISIONS

45+ SWEET AND SAVORY RECIPES

CASSIE WINSLOW

photographs by NAOMI MCCOLLOCH

CHRONICLE BOOKS

SAN FRANCISCO

Library of Congress Cataloging-in-Publication Data

Names: Winslow, Cassie, author. | McColloch, Naomi, photographer.
Title: Floral provisions : 45+ sweet and savory recipes / Cassie Winslow ; photographs by Naomi McColloch.
Description: San Francisco, California : Chronicle Books, 2021. | Includes index.
Identifiers: LCCN 2021025838 | ISBN 9781797204598
Subjects: LCSH: Cooking (Flowers) | LCGFT: Cookbooks.
Classification: LCC TX814.5.F5 W56 2021 | DDC 641.6/59--dc23
LC record available at https://lccn.loc.gov/2021025838

Manufactured in China.

Design by Vanessa Dina.

Etsy is a registered trademark of Etsy, Inc. Immaculate Baking Co. is a registered trademark of Immaculate Baking LLC and is the intellectual property of General Mills. Pink Lady is a registered trademark of Carlton Fruit Trees, Inc. St. Germain is a registered trademark of Bacardi & Company Limited Corporation. TCHO is a registered trademark of Tcho Ventures, Inc. Terrain is a registered trademark of Urban Outfitters Wholesale, Inc.

10 9 8 7 6 5 4 3 2

Chronicle books and gifts are available at special quantity discounts to corporations, professional associations, literacy programs, and other organizations. For details and discount information, please contact our premiums department at corporatesales@chroniclebooks.com or at 1-800-759-0190.

Chronicle Books LLC
680 Second Street
San Francisco, California 94107
www.chroniclebooks.com

TO NICHOLAS AND CHARLOTTE,
THE LOVES OF MY LIFE

AND TO ALL OF THOSE WHO HAVE AN
INSATIABLE PASSION FOR FLOWERS . . .

CONTENTS

INTRODUCTION

I remember one of the very first times I used edible flowers in the kitchen . . . I had found some culinary lavender at the Ferry Building farmers' market in San Francisco. It was the middle of summer and the wild blackberries were bursting throughout our property. My husband picked so many blackberries, they were spilling out of the giant mixing bowl he so lovingly brought into the kitchen. I decided to improvise and made homemade blackberry lavender jam and a blackberry lavender crumble. The flavor combination was intoxicating. When I tasted each one, I didn't notice an overwhelming lavender flavor, just a touch of something special that made the jam and crumble so different from anything I had ever whipped up before. The lavender added a touch of elegance and a flavor that made me gasp. It was absolutely wonderful, and thus started my culinary adventure with edible flowers.

This book is full of my favorite edible flower recipes from experimenting over the years: Rose Petal French Toast (page 43), Apricot Chamomile Jam (page 26), Rose Geranium Ice Cream (page 124), and Floral Doughnuts Four Ways (page 60) just to name a few. You're about to make some of the most beautiful delights you've ever tasted.

In this book, you'll find ways to use edible flowers in brunch recipes, afternoon tea goodies, and desserts, with just a few floral beverages thrown in for good measure.

A floral pantry chapter in the beginning is full of recipes for staples that allow you to easily make many of the treats in this book and experiment on your own by adding a pantry item to something unexpected when you feel inspired. Maybe it's a sprinkling of Chamomile Salt (page 14) atop a poached egg, a touch of Lavender Syrup (page 21) in your evening glass of rosé, or a dollop of Rose Geranium and Strawberry Jam (page 23) in your morning smoothie. Adding edible flowers to your favorite everyday dishes is a pleasing way to add a little fanciness to everyday life.

I hope I inspire you to experiment with edible flowers in the kitchen by adding bits of blooms here and there. If you aren't able to get your hands on a particular flower a recipe calls for, use what you are able to source (for sourcing tips, see page 96). I have found that this is the best way to make something your own, and it may even end up being a superior flavor combination than the original!

So have fun, experiment, and enjoy the delight of edible flowers.

BLOOMS ON MY TABLE

Pillowy thoughts of lilacs and sugar

Melted, blended, stirred

Warming florals toasted and bare

Rose petals and lavender floating in air

A taste, a sprinkle

Butter, a jam

A bouquet of floral confetti

Baking in color

Garnished with blooms

The cake is almost ready

The chamomile sings, the pansies delight

The buttercream tastes delicious

A joyous heartbeat, a gorgeous display

And the art of botanical bliss

FLORAL

CHAPTER 1

PANTRY

Chamomile Salt / **14**

Rose Salt / **15**

Jasmine Sugar / **18**

Garden Party Sugar / **19**

Floral Butter / **20**

Lavender Syrup / **21**

Rose Geranium Syrup / **22**

Rose Geranium + Strawberry Jam / **23**

Apricot Chamomile Jam / **26**

Floral Infused Honey / **27**

Orange Blossom Chocolate Hazelnut Spread / **28**

CHAMOMILE SALT

¼ **cup [5 g] dried chamomile**

½ **cup [100 g] fine sea salt**

I had a feeling the combination of chamomile and salt could be really exceptional, but I had no idea just how delicious and versatile this pantry staple could be. Chamomile is such a dynamic flavor; you can add it to both sweet and savory recipes since it has both a sweet and an herbaceous flavor.

MAKES APPROXIMATELY
½ CUP [105 G]

In a food processor or spice grinder, grind the chamomile until it resembles small flakes, about 10 seconds. Be sure not to grind it into a powder.

In a small bowl, stir together the salt and chamomile. For optimal flavor, wait about 1 week before using, though you can use immediately if needed. Store in an airtight container at room temperature for up to 6 months.

ROSE SALT

¼ cup [5 g] dried rose petals

½ cup [100 g] fine sea salt

Rose Salt is one of my favorite ingredients of all time. The first time I made it, I was actually putting together a luxurious bath soak. But I realized after mixing the salt with the organic dried rose petals that I had made a wonderful culinary ingredient. That night, I sprinkled our homemade French fries with this gorgeous creation and the following day, I used it as a finishing touch to rim an afternoon margarita. I always have it in a pretty glass jar on my kitchen counter and find a new way to use it daily.

MAKES APPROXIMATELY
½ CUP [105 G]

In a food processor or spice grinder, grind the rose petals for 5 to 10 seconds, checking the petals regularly until they resemble small flakes. Be sure not to grind them into a powder.

In a small bowl, stir together the salt and rose petals. For optimal flavor, wait about 1 week before using, though you can use immediately if needed. Store in an airtight container at room temperature for up to 1 year.

JASMINE SUGAR

¼ cup [15 g] fragrant jasmine tea leaves

¾ cup [150 g] granulated sugar

Jasmine has stolen my heart. This sweet-smelling, delicate bloom can be found in dried form in a variety of teas, and it is able to bring so many different ingredients to life. From syrups to baked goods, jasmine is wonderfully aromatic and tastes just as wonderful as it smells. I can't wait to introduce you to this glorious ingredient, if you haven't yet had the pleasure.

MAKES APPROXIMATELY
¾ CUP [165 G]

In a food processor or spice grinder, gently blend the jasmine tea by pulsing until the blooms resemble small sprinkles. In a small bowl, stir together the jasmine and sugar until well combined. Store in an airtight container at room temperature for up to 4 months.

GARDEN PARTY SUGAR

1 Tbsp dried hibiscus

1 Tbsp dried chamomile

1 Tbsp dried lavender

1 Tbsp dried rose petals

1 Tbsp dried calendula

1 cup [200 g] cane sugar

This sugar is like nature's confetti. A blend of some of my favorite edible flowers, this colorful combination of blooms is so much fun to use in baked goods, especially cakes (see page 111). I also love making it into a syrup that can be used in homemade coffee creamer for a fun weekend coffee bar situation (see page 69).

MAKES APPROXIMATELY
1¼ CUPS [210 G]

In a food processor or spice grinder, pulse the hibiscus, chamomile, lavender, rose petals, and calendula until the flowers resemble small flakes. Be sure not to grind them into a powder.

In a small bowl, stir together the flowers and the sugar. For optimal flavor, wait about 1 week before using. However, you can absolutely use the sugar immediately, the flavor will just be a bit more subtle. Store in an airtight container at room temperature for up to 2 months.

FLORAL BUTTER

½ cup [110 g] unsalted butter, at room temperature

1 Tbsp fresh edible flower petals (such as pansies, calendula, chamomile, or nasturtium)

Imagine the most beautiful butter you've ever seen . . . sprinkled with colorful, floral confetti. Floral butters will make your favorite dish sing. Serve on top of stacks of crepes or on your favorite baguette from a local bakery.

MAKES APPROXIMATELY ½ CUP [110 G]

In a medium mixing bowl, combine the butter and fresh edible flower petals with a rubber spatula, gently folding the petals into the butter until just combined. You want to be very gentle during this process or you will break down the flowers too much and it won't look as pretty. Scoop the mixture into a small bowl and press it down to form one solid piece. Store, covered, in the refrigerator and use within a few days.

NOTE: You can use dried blooms to make floral butters too! I love making Lavender Butter and Rose Butter using dried flowers since the flavor is stronger than when using fresh blooms. It's best to use a food processor to help break down the dried blooms a bit first. Pulse the butter and dried petals until combined, about 5 to 10 pulses total. Scoop the mixture into a small bowl and press it down to form one solid piece. Store, covered, in the refrigerator for up to 1 week.

LAVENDER SYRUP

1 cup [200 g] granulated sugar

¼ cup [10 g] lavender petals

Lavender has a special place in my heart, as it was one of the first edible flowers I started experimenting with years ago. This syrup has become a staple in my pantry and I use it for so many goodies. It's great in cocktails and iced coffee, especially in the middle of winter when you are dreaming of spring blooms. I also love to drizzle it over chocolate ice cream and pancakes (see page 48).

MAKES 1 CUP [240 ML]

In a small saucepan over medium heat, stir together the sugar, lavender, and ½ cup [120 ml] of filtered water. Stir occasionally until the sugar has completely dissolved and the mixture has thickened into a syrup, about 5 minutes. Remove from the heat and let cool for 5 minutes.

Strain the mixture through a fine-mesh sieve set over a small bowl, then transfer the syrup to an airtight container. Store in the refrigerator for up to 1 week.

ROSE GERANIUM SYRUP

1 cup [200 g] cane sugar

5 fresh organic rose geranium leaves

Rose geranium is divine; the fragrance is so beautiful. I love adding this syrup to smoothies for a touch of sweetness. It's also wonderful to use at brunch drizzled over French toast (see page 43). Or add it to a daisy cocktail for an exceptional treat (see page 93).

MAKES 1 CUP [240 ML]

In a small saucepan over medium heat, stir together the sugar, rose geranium leaves, and ½ cup [120 ml] of filtered water. Stir occasionally until the sugar has completely dissolved and the mixture has thickened into a syrup, about 5 minutes. Remove from the heat and let cool for 5 minutes.

Discard the rose geranium leaves, then transfer the syrup to an airtight container. Store in the refrigerator for up to 1 week.

ROSE GERANIUM + STRAWBERRY JAM

12 oz [340 g] quartered fresh strawberries

⅔ cup [160 ml] Rose Geranium Syrup (facing page)

2 Tbsp freshly squeezed lemon juice

Strawberries and rose geranium are my favorite combination. They harmonize with one another in such an enchanting way. This jam is a lovely way to allow this pair to show off their magic. Slather it on a piece of sourdough toast covered in butter or layer it with almond butter for an indulgent sandwich.

MAKES ABOUT 1 CUP [300 G]

In a small saucepan over medium heat, add the strawberries, syrup, and lemon juice. Bring to a simmer and lower the heat slightly. Simmer for about 5 minutes until the strawberries soften. Using a potato masher, mash the strawberries to break them down a bit. Continue to simmer over low heat for 20 to 30 minutes. Keep an eye on the jam and lower the heat as needed. You want it to gently simmer, so if it starts to boil, lower the heat.

Transfer the jam to a large, heatproof container, such as a mason jar, and let cool on the counter for about 1 hour. Cover and store in the refrigerator for up to 3 weeks.

APRICOT CHAMOMILE JAM

1½ **Tbsp dried chamomile**

2¼ **cups [215 g] ripe apricots, sliced**

⅓ **cup [65 g] granulated sugar**

2 **Tbsp freshly squeezed lemon juice**

This fragrant jam is one of my favorite summertime treats. Apricots and chamomile complement each other in such a delightful way. I love slathering some atop a layer of ricotta on sourdough toast and sprinkling it with chopped pistachios (see page 83); it's the perfect summer snack. You can also dollop some on your favorite vanilla ice cream for a refreshing dessert on a sizzling day.

MAKES ABOUT I CUP [300 G]

In a spice grinder or food processor, grind the chamomile flowers until the blooms resemble small flakes or sprinkles. This happens very quickly so you only need to pulse a few times.

In a medium saucepan over medium heat, add the chamomile, apricots, ½ cup [120 ml] of filtered water, the sugar, and lemon juice. Using a wooden spoon, mix until combined. Allow the mixture to simmer for about 5 minutes until the apricots begin to break down and soften. Using a potato masher, mash the apricot slices in the mixture to help break them down. The mixture should be syrupy. Lower the heat to medium-low and simmer for another 10 minutes until it looks glossy and thick. Remove from the heat.

TIP: Jams are flexible! If you make a jam and it's too thick, return the mixture to the saucepan over medium heat and add 1 Tbsp at a time of either lemon juice or water, and simmer until the desired consistency is reached. If the mixture is too thin, you can either use it as a sauce instead or add another ¼ cup of sliced fruit and 1 Tbsp of sugar to the mixture. Return the saucepan to medium heat and simmer until glossy and thick. Have fun!

Transfer the jam to a large, heatproof container, such as a mason jar, and let cool on the counter for about 1 hour. Cover and store in the refrigerator for up to 3 weeks.

FLORAL INFUSED HONEY

10 oz [280 g] honey

2 Tbsp dried chamomile

2 Tbsp dried rose petals

This rose petal and chamomile–infused honey is another staple in my pantry. I love to use it in my tea or coffee, drizzle it on top of almond butter toast (see page 82), and even serve it on a cheese board when I have guests over for afternoon tea (see page 72).

MAKES ⅔ CUP [230 G]

In a medium saucepan, combine all of the ingredients with 3 Tbsp of filtered water. Place the saucepan over medium heat and bring the mixture to a gentle simmer. Allow it to simmer for 1 to 2 minutes, then remove the saucepan from the heat and allow the honey to steep for 7 minutes.

Strain the honey through a fine-mesh sieve into a medium bowl with a spout or a 2 cup [480 ml] glass pitcher. Transfer to a glass jar with a lid and store at room temperature for up to 1 month.

ORANGE BLOSSOM CHOCOLATE HAZELNUT SPREAD

1 cup [120 g] raw hazelnuts, toasted and cooled

¾ cup [75 g] sifted confectioners' sugar

¼ cup [20 g] Dutch-processed cocoa powder

¼ tsp Rose Salt (page 15)

1 Tbsp orange blossom water

¼ cup plus 2 Tbsp [85 g] melted and cooled coconut oil (unflavored)

Homemade chocolate hazelnut spread is a delight indeed and the orange blossom water adds a special floral note to elevate this pantry staple. Slather it on crepes, spread it on sourdough toast, or add to a vanilla milkshake.

MAKES APPROXIMATELY 1 CUP [230 G]

Place the hazelnuts in a food processor and process until fine—this takes about 5 minutes. Add the confectioners' sugar, cocoa powder, Rose Salt, and orange blossom water. Process and slowly add the coconut oil. Continue processing for another 3 minutes or until the mixture is smooth, stopping to scrape down the sides of the food processor bowl with a rubber spatula as needed. Store the spread in an airtight container, such as a mason jar, at room temperature for up to 1 week.

USING EDIBLE FLOWERS IN EVERYDAY RECIPES

ADD FRESH EDIBLE FLOWER PETALS TO EVERYDAY RECIPES

Sprinkle in pancake (see page 48), waffle (see page 45), and crepe batter. Add to homemade tortilla, flatbread, and pizza dough.

Want to add more color to your salad? Add a handful of colorful flower petals to your salad mix for a vibrant, eye-catching dish. You can also add them to your favorite salad dressing.

Mix fresh blooms into softened, spreadable cheeses, such as cream cheese (see page 88), goat cheese (see page 86), and ricotta. Add to softened butter, both salted and unsalted (see page 20).

ADD DRIED FLOWERS TO EVERYDAY RECIPES

Add to salts (see pages 14 and 15) and sugars (see pages 18 and 19), and let infuse for about 1 week.

Add to simple syrups (see page 21) and jams (see page 26) for a floral treat.

Use in homemade ice cream (see page 124) or frosting for your favorite cake. Add to icings for cookies or doughnuts (see page 60). Add to confectioners' sugar to sprinkle atop a delightful dessert (see page 50).

Add to smoothies, milkshakes, and your favorite blended margarita.

Chamomile Salt (page 14) and Rose Salt
(page 15) make a surprising and beautiful rim
for any libation. You can also sprinkle these
colorful salts on everyday favorites, such as
eggs, potatoes, nuts, cookies, and pasta dishes.
I love using the Rose Salt on French fries and
the Chamomile Salt on hamburger patties or
to season fried chicken. Season salad dress-
ings, sauces, and marinades with these unique
pantry staples.

Jasmine Sugar (page 18) and Garden Party
Sugar (page 19) can be substituted for regular
sugar in many of your favorite baked goods,
such as cookies, cakes, brownies, scones,
and pies.

Lavender Syrup (page 21), Rose Geranium
Syrup (page 22), and Floral Infused Honey
(page 27) can be drizzled on top of your
favorite ice cream and breakfast favorites. Use
these syrups to sweeten your morning tea or
coffee or to shake up a cocktail in the evening.
You can add it to sparkling wine for a floral
mimosa too!

Rose Geranium and Strawberry Jam (page 23)
and Apricot Chamomile Jam (page 26) both
make for a sensational PB&J. Serve them on
a cheese board (see page 74) or in a smoothie.
Dollop some on top of scones (see page 90)
or biscuits, or use them to sweeten whipped
creams or flavor homemade ice creams. My
favorite? Slather them on top of toast for the
ultimate morning snack (see page 82).

FLORAL

CHAPTER 2

BRUNCH

Homemade Chamomile Granola
+ Hibiscus Parfaits / **34**

Lavender Crepes with Lavender Pluot Sauce / **37**

Jasmine + White Peach Muffins / **40**

Rose Petal French Toast with Rose Butter
+ Rose Geranium Syrup / **43**

Calendula Sourdough Waffles with Nasturtium
Butter + Floral Infused Honey / **45**

Garden Party Pancakes with Lavender Syrup / **48**

Ebleskiver with Rose Confectioners' Sugar / **50**

Blueberry Lilac Dutch Baby / **53**

Plum Lavender Clafoutis / **56**

Jasmine Sticky Buns / **59**

Floral Doughnuts Four Ways / **60**

Calendula, Gouda + Bacon Quiche
with Fresh Blooming Herbs / **66**

Coffee with Garden Party Creamer / **69**

HOMEMADE CHAMOMILE GRANOLA + HIBISCUS PARFAITS

HOMEMADE CHAMOMILE GRANOLA

4 cups [400 g] rolled oats

1 cup [120 g] chopped walnuts

⅓ cup [80 ml] organic canola oil

¼ cup [85 g] honey or Floral Infused Honey (page 27)

1 Tbsp unsalted butter, melted

1 Tbsp dried chamomile

½ tsp Rose Salt (page 15)

¼ cup [35 g] dried currants

HIBISCUS SYRUP

½ cup [100 g] granulated sugar

2 tsp dried hibiscus

PARFAITS

3 cups [720 g] Greek yogurt

1 to 2 cups [120 to 240 g] sliced fruit

Handful of borage petals or other edible flowers, for garnish (optional)

I love creating these beautiful parfaits as meal prep for the week—they make a pretty fancy weekday breakfast. I layer the ingredients in mason jars and store them in the refrigerator so I can grab one for breakfast on days when I'm rushing out the door. The color of the hibiscus syrup alone will make your heart skip a beat. You can make these year-round by using your favorite in-season fruit; I love to use apples, berries, and stone fruit, especially white nectarines.

MAKES 4 PARFAITS

To make the granola: Preheat the oven to 350°F [180°C].

In a large mixing bowl, add the oats, walnuts, oil, honey, butter, chamomile, and Rose Salt. Mix until well combined. Transfer the mixture to a baking sheet and spread it out evenly using a rubber spatula.

Place the sheet in the middle rack of the oven and bake for 30 minutes, checking it every 10 minutes and mixing the granola to ensure it bakes evenly. It can be helpful to use a metal spatula when doing this to remove any sticky bits from the baking sheet.

CONTINUE

For a fresh floral yogurt: Gently mix 3 Tbsp of fresh petals into every 1 cup [240 g] of yogurt for an even more colorful treat.

For hibiscus yogurt: Omit the hibiscus syrup as a drizzle in this recipe and instead mix it directly into the yogurt. It's delicious on its own or served with fresh fruit!

Once the granola is a toasty, golden brown, remove it from the oven and sprinkle the dried currants on top of the granola. Let cool for 30 minutes. Transfer the granola to an airtight container of your choice (I like to use a large glass jar) and store at room temperature for up to 1 week.

To make the syrup: In a small saucepan over medium heat, stir together the sugar, hibiscus, and ¼ cup [60 ml] of filtered water. Stir occasionally until the sugar has completely dissolved and the mixture has thickened into a syrup, about 5 minutes. Remove from the heat and allow the hibiscus to steep in the syrup for an additional 5 minutes. Strain the syrup through a fine-mesh sieve into a small bowl and let cool completely. Transfer to a glass jar with an airtight lid. Store in the refrigerator for 1 to 2 weeks.

To make the parfaits: In a 16 oz [480 ml] mason jar, layer 3 Tbsp of the granola, ¼ cup [60 g] of the yogurt, and 1 Tbsp of the hibiscus syrup. Place a few slices of fruit atop the syrup, then repeat the layering steps, starting with the granola, until you run out of space in your jar. I am typically able to fit three layers into a mason jar of this size, depending on which fruit I use. Top with extra fruit, a drizzle of hibiscus syrup, and the flower petals, if using.

LAVENDER CREPES WITH LAVENDER PLUOT SAUCE

LAVENDER PLUOT SAUCE

2 cups [335 g] sliced pluots (you can also use plums or your favorite stone fruit)

3 Tbsp granulated sugar

1 Tbsp freshly squeezed lemon juice

½ tsp dried lavender

LAVENDER CREPES

6 Tbsp [85 g] Lavender Butter (page 20), plus 1 tsp to grease the pan

2 cups [480 ml] whole milk

1½ cups [210 g] all-purpose flour

2 large eggs

½ tsp Rose Salt (page 15)

1 tsp confectioners' sugar, for serving

Imagine a bed of warm crepes served with a pat of lavender butter and topped with a tangy and vibrant pluot sauce. It's one of my favorite breakfasts to make on a Monday morning. You can make the batter the night before and allow it to set in the refrigerator overnight so that you can start the week with a belly full of beautiful food and a skip in your step.

MAKES 8 CREPES

To make the sauce: In a medium saucepan over medium heat, add the pluots, ¼ cup [60 ml] of filtered water, the sugar, lemon juice, and dried lavender. Using a wooden spoon, stir until the mixture comes to a simmer. Simmer for 8 to 10 minutes, stirring occasionally. Once the mixture has reached a sauce-like thickness, remove the saucepan from the heat and allow the mixture to cool for about 10 minutes. Store in an airtight container in the refrigerator and enjoy within a few days.

To make the crepes: Melt and cool 2 Tbsp of the Lavender Butter. In a large mixing bowl, whisk together the milk, flour, eggs, the melted Lavender Butter, and the Rose Salt until smooth. Pour the batter through a fine-mesh sieve into another large bowl, using a rubber spatula to work the batter through the sieve. Cover and let the

CONTINUED

TIP: This sauce is also quite heavenly when poured over Rose Geranium Ice Cream (page 124).

batter sit in the refrigerator for at least 1 hour or up to overnight.

Place an 8 in [20 cm] nonstick crepe pan over medium heat and lightly grease the pan using 1 tsp of Lavender Butter. Pour ⅓ cup [80 ml] of batter into the pan and try to make the crepes as thin as you can by tilting the pan so that the batter spreads to cover the whole pan bottom evenly. Let cook for 1 to 2 minutes until little golden dots begin to form, flip, then cook for 1 or 2 minutes more. Repeat with the remaining batter.

Serve immediately with the Lavender Pluot Sauce and the remaining 4 Tbsp [55 g] of Lavender Butter. Use a small fine-mesh sieve to sprinkle the confectioners' sugar over the top of the crepes.

JASMINE + WHITE PEACH MUFFINS

1¼ cups [150 g] sifted all-purpose flour

1 tsp baking powder

½ tsp Chamomile Salt (page 14)

¼ tsp baking soda

½ cup [110 g] Jasmine Sugar (page 18), plus 1 Tbsp for sprinkling

¼ cup [55 g] Rose Butter (page 20), melted and cooled

1 large egg

½ cup [120 g] crème fraîche

1 Tbsp mascarpone

1 tsp vanilla extract

1¾ cups [230 g] sliced white peaches

How lovely your house will smell when baking these sweet-scented muffins! I prefer making the batter the night before and baking these beauties in the oven right when I wake up in the morning—just let the batter sit out for 30 minutes prior to baking to take off the chill. By the time my morning cuppa is ready to sip, I have a scrumptious muffin speckled with jasmine and layered with floral flavors waiting for me to devour.

MAKES 10 MUFFINS

Preheat the oven to 400°F [200°C].

In a medium mixing bowl, whisk together the flour, baking powder, Chamomile Salt, and baking soda until well combined. Set aside.

In a large mixing bowl, whisk together the Jasmine Sugar and Rose Butter until well combined. Add the egg and whisk until combined. Add the crème fraîche, mascarpone, and vanilla. Whisk until just combined.

Add the dry mixture to the wet mixture. Using a rubber spatula, mix until just combined. Add the sliced peaches and gently fold with the spatula until just combined. Allow the mixture to sit at room temperature for about 10 minutes.

CONTINUED

These muffins are also lovely with apples in the middle of autumn. Simply swap the white peaches for your favorite tart apple! Pink Lady apples are wonderful in these muffins . . . just be sure to peel the apples first.

Line a standard muffin tin with cupcake liners. Using an ice cream scoop or large spoon, dollop about ¼ cup [60 ml] of batter into each cup. Sprinkle each with a pinch of Jasmine Sugar and bake for about 17 minutes or until the tops are golden and a toothpick inserted into the center of a muffin comes out clean.

Transfer the muffins to a wire rack and let cool for 5 to 10 minutes before serving. Be sure the muffins are completely cool before transferring to an airtight container to store at room temperature for up to 2 days.

ROSE PETAL FRENCH TOAST WITH ROSE BUTTER + ROSE GERANIUM SYRUP

2 Tbsp dried rose petals

4 Tbsp [55 g] Rose Butter (page 20)

2 large eggs

1 cup [240 ml] whole milk

1 tsp vanilla extract

½ tsp ground cinnamon

4 slices brioche, challah, or your favorite loaf

Rose Geranium Syrup (page 22), for serving

Fresh garden roses, for garnish (optional)

T I P : I love serving this dish with crispy bacon and drizzling the bacon with a touch of Rose Geranium Syrup (about 1 Tbsp of syrup per dozen bacon strips). It's simply scrumptious.

Layering both savory and sweet floral flavors, this special recipe is a fun way to surprise guests for breakfast. I love using brioche in this recipe, but feel free to use your favorite loaf. Soaked in a rose petal custard, then layered with Rose Butter and topped with Rose Geranium Syrup, this recipe takes French toast to a whole new level of goodness.

SERVES 2 (MAKES 4 PIECES OF FRENCH TOAST)

Using a mortar and pestle or spice grinder, gently grind the rose petals until they resemble small flakes. Set aside.

In a large cast-iron skillet over medium heat, melt 1 Tbsp of the Rose Butter. In a large mixing bowl, whisk together the rose petals, eggs, milk, vanilla, and cinnamon until combined.

Place a slice of the bread in the batter and let soak until it is saturated, 1 to 2 minutes. Once the butter has melted in the skillet, add the slice of bread. Cook for 2 to 3 minutes on each side. Repeat with the rest of the bread slices.

CONTINUED

Serve immediately or keep warm on a baking sheet in an oven preheated to 325°F [165°C]. Serve with the remaining 3 Tbsp of Rose Butter and drizzle with Rose Geranium Syrup. Garnish each plate with a fresh garden rose or sprinkle them with fresh rose petals if you fancy.

CALENDULA SOURDOUGH WAFFLES WITH NASTURTIUM BUTTER + FLORAL INFUSED HONEY

2 large eggs

1½ cups [180 g] sifted all-purpose flour

1 cup [240 ml] room temperature sourdough starter

2 Tbsp granulated sugar

½ tsp Rose Salt (page 15)

3 Tbsp unsalted butter, melted and cooled, plus more for greasing the waffle iron

¼ tsp baking soda

3 Tbsp fresh calendula petals

½ cup [110 g] Nasturtium Butter (page 20), for serving

½ cup [120 ml] Floral Infused Honey (page 27), for serving

Whenever my family went to visit my grandmother when I was growing up, she would be sure to make us a batch of her sourdough waffles. I can still smell the tangy sourdough batter and see the steam coming from her waffle iron as we sat and waited to devour them. Her sourdough starter continues to be kept alive in our family, mostly by making a batch of these waffles quite often. I'm sure she would be delighted by the addition of floral butter and honey.

The starter I use has been in my family for over forty years, but you can easily find sourdough starters at local natural foods stores or even online if this is a new adventure for you.

A note on sourdough starter: The night before you'd like to make these scrumptious waffles, you will need to feed your sourdough starter. Feed it as you normally would, or according to the instructions you received with it, making sure to add enough flour and water that you will have 1 cup [240 ml] of starter to use for this recipe. Cover and let sit out at room temperature overnight. It should be bubbly when you check on it in the morning.

CONTINUED

Separate the egg yolks from the whites. Reserve the yolks, and place the whites in the bowl of a stand mixer fitted with the whisk attachment. Beat the egg whites on medium speed until stiff peaks form.

In a large mixing bowl, mix together the flour, sourdough starter, and ¾ cup [180 ml] of filtered water until just combined. Add the egg yolks, sugar, Rose Salt, butter, and baking soda. Mix until just combined. Using a rubber spatula, gently fold in the egg whites and calendula petals.

Now it's time to make the waffles. Using a waffle maker, cook the waffles according to the manufacturer's instructions. I like to lightly brush my waffle iron with melted butter before I add the batter for each waffle. I use about ¾ to 1 cup [180 to 240 ml] of batter for each waffle, but this can vary depending on the size of your waffle maker.

Serve immediately with a pat of the Nasturtium Butter and a drizzling of the Floral Infused Honey.

GARDEN PARTY PANCAKES WITH LAVENDER SYRUP

2 cups [240 g] sifted
all-purpose flour

1 tsp baking soda

1 tsp baking powder

2½ cups [600 ml] whole milk

4 Tbsp [40 g] Garden
Party Sugar (page 19)

1 large egg

8 tsp unsalted butter,
melted and slightly cooled

½ cup [110 g] Floral Butter
(page 20), for serving

1 cup [240 ml] Lavender
Syrup (page 21), for serving

A handful of fresh blooms
(such as lavender or garden
roses), for garnish

These Garden Party Pancakes are a fun way to reinvent your favorite weekend breakfast. Filled with calendula, hibiscus, lavender, rose, and chamomile, it's a breakfast bouquet with the best floral layers. Top with Floral Butter (page 20) and Lavender Syrup (page 21) for the ultimate celebration of the delights edible flowers can bring.

SERVES 4

(MAKES ABOUT 10 PANCAKES)

In a large mixing bowl, whisk together the flour, baking soda, and baking powder until just combined. In a medium mixing bowl, whisk together the milk, 2 Tbsp of the Garden Party Sugar, the egg, and 2 tsp of the melted butter until just combined. Add the wet mixture to the dry mixture and whisk together until just combined.

In a large cast-iron skillet over medium-high heat, warm 2 tsp of the butter. Once the skillet is hot, you can start making the pancakes, about three per batch at ¼ cup [60 ml] of batter each. After about 2 minutes, the sides of the pancakes should start to bubble up, which means it is time to flip! Using a metal spatula, flip the pancakes and cook for another 2 minutes.

Continue this process until all of the batter has been used up and you have about ten pancakes. Serve immediately with a pat of Floral Butter, a drizzle of Lavender Syrup, and a sprinkle of the remaining 2 Tbsp of Garden Party Sugar. Garnish each plate with a fresh bloom.

EBLESKIVER WITH ROSE CONFECTIONERS' SUGAR

3 large eggs

¼ tsp cream of tartar

1¾ cups plus 2 Tbsp [450 ml] whole milk

2 Tbsp lemon juice, freshly squeezed

2 cups [240 g] sifted all-purpose flour

2 tsp granulated sugar or Jasmine Sugar (page 18)

1 tsp baking powder

1 tsp baking soda

½ tsp Rose Salt (page 15)

½ cup [120 ml] organic canola oil

1 Tbsp dried rose petals

¼ cup [25 g] sifted confectioners' sugar

¼ cup [75 g] Rose Geranium and Strawberry Jam (page 23) or Apricot Chamomile Jam (page 26), for serving

Every Christmas morning since I was a little babe, my mom would make ebleskiver (or aebleskiver, depending on how you spell it) after we opened up our presents and were recovering from the chaos. She would serve them with confectioners' sugar and some wonderful homemade jam. Sometimes we would invite friends over, and it was so much fun to see them tasting ebleskiver for the first time. They're sort of like a doughnut but somehow more sophisticated. They're so light and fluffy. I just love them . . . and the pan you cook them in is the cutest. I now get to continue the family tradition and make them for my daughter every Christmas morning, smelling and tasting the nostalgia with every bite. Thank you to my mother for letting me share this special family recipe—with my own floral spin, of course.

SERVES 8

Separate the egg yolks from the whites. Reserve the yolks, and place the whites in the bowl of a stand mixer fitted with the whisk attachment. Beat the egg whites and cream of tartar on medium speed until stiff peaks form. Set aside.

In a small bowl, mix together the milk and lemon juice. Set aside.

CONTINUED

In a large mixing bowl, whisk together the flour, granulated sugar, baking powder, baking soda, and Rose Salt until well blended. Add the milk mixture and the egg yolks to the flour mixture. Whisk together until well combined. Using a rubber spatula, gently fold in the egg whites until the mixture is well blended. Be careful not to overmix.

Place a petite ebleskiver pan over medium heat. Fill each cup in the pan a little less than halfway with oil. Once the oil is hot (be extra careful), add about 2 Tbsp of the batter to each cup in the pan. Let cook until the bottoms are golden, 3 to 4 minutes (and even faster once you get rolling), then, using a fork, gently flip each one and cook for another 2 to 3 minutes. When the ebleskiver are done, place them on a paper towel to drain any excess oil.

Using a mortar and pestle or a spice grinder, grind the rose petals until flake form (this happens very quickly if using a spice grinder). In a small mixing bowl, mix together the rose petals and confectioners' sugar until well combined.

Serve the ebleskiver warm with the rose-sugar mixture sprinkled on top and the jam alongside.

BLUEBERRY LILAC DUTCH BABY

½ cup [120 ml] whole milk

2 large eggs

½ cup [60 g] sifted all-purpose flour

2 Tbsp fresh organic lilac blooms, plus 2 Tbsp for garnish

2 Tbsp granulated sugar or Jasmine Sugar (page 18)

¼ tsp Rose Salt (page 15) or Chamomile Salt (page 14)

1 Tbsp unsalted butter

⅔ cup [90 g] blueberries

1 Tbsp confectioners' sugar, for serving

2 to 3 Tbsp Floral Infused Honey (page 27), for serving

The first time I made a Dutch baby, I thought I was doing something wrong because it seemed way too easy to throw together. It turns out I wasn't doing anything wrong, it's just that easy. Over the past decade, I've made so many that I've lost count. The combinations are never-ending, but blueberry and lilac make a charming pair. Lilac season is so fleeting that I'm always tossing these flowers in this or that while they're around, and really, they taste good in nearly everything. Lilac blooms make such a gorgeous garnish too. Such a delightful springtime treat.

SERVES 2

Preheat the oven to 400°F [200°C].

In a blender, add the milk, eggs, flour, lilac blooms, granulated sugar, and Rose Salt. Blend until well combined, about 1 minute. Set aside.

In two separate 6½ in [16.5 cm] cast-iron skillets over medium heat, melt ½ Tbsp of butter. Once melted, divide the batter between the two skillets and add a handful of blueberries to each one. Place the skillets in the oven and bake for 15 to 18 minutes or until the center is set and the edges are golden brown.

CONTINUED

MAKE A YUMMY FLORAL BERRY SAUCE TO SERVE WITH YOUR DUTCH BABY

In a small saucepan over medium heat, place ¼ cup [35 g] of fresh blueberries, 2 Tbsp of your favorite jam, 1 tsp of your favorite bloom (I love using jasmine here), and 2 Tbsp of filtered water. Bring to a simmer for about 5 minutes. Remove from the heat and let cool for about 5 minutes. Pour the sauce into a pretty, small syrup pitcher to serve alongside your Dutch baby.

Garnish each skillet with more fresh blueberries, and, using a fine-mesh sieve, sprinkle with confectioners' sugar. Scatter the remaining 2 Tbsp of lilac blooms over the top, and drizzle with the Floral Infused Honey. Serve immediately.

PLUM LAVENDER CLAFOUTIS

1 tsp unsalted butter, for greasing the skillet

15 oz [430 g] sliced plums

⅔ cup [130 g] granulated sugar

4 large eggs

½ cup [70 g] all-purpose flour

1 tsp crushed lavender petals

¼ tsp Rose Salt (page 15) or Chamomile Salt (page 14)

1½ cups [360 ml] whole milk

1 tsp vanilla extract

1 Tbsp confectioners' sugar

TIP: If you're feeling extra fancy, make hibiscus confectioners' sugar. In a small bowl, simply mix ½ tsp of ground dried hibiscus petals with the confectioners' sugar until combined. Using a fine-mesh sieve, sprinkle over the clafoutis.

Have you ever made a clafoutis? Making it just to be able to say the name is fun enough. It's also super easy to whip up since it takes less than 10 minutes to make the batter. The end result is so delicious and pretty, and it's the perfect way to use up any leftover fruit, especially in the middle of summer. And pairing lavender with stone fruit? A match made in heaven.

SERVES 4

Preheat the oven to 350°F [180°C]. Evenly butter the bottom and sides of a large cast-iron skillet.

In a large mixing bowl, toss the plums with half of the granulated sugar. Assemble the plums in the cast-iron skillet however you fancy. In the same large mixing bowl, whisk together the eggs, flour, lavender, Rose Salt, and the remaining granulated sugar until well blended. Add the milk and vanilla and whisk until just combined.

Pour the mixture into the skillet over the plums and bake for about 50 minutes or until just set. Let cool for about 10 minutes. Using a fine-mesh sieve, sprinkle confectioners' sugar over the top. Serve immediately.

JASMINE STICKY BUNS

¼ cup [50 g] packed dark brown sugar

8 Tbsp [115 g] unsalted butter, melted

2 tsp organic light corn syrup or golden syrup

¼ cup [55 g] Jasmine Sugar (page 18)

¼ tsp ground cinnamon

One 15 oz [425 g] carton biscuit dough (I love to use Immaculate Baking Co.'s Flaky Biscuits)

The delight that these sticky buns bring is inexplicable—they are just divine. Every time I bake them, they are gobbled up.

SERVES 8

Preheat the oven to 350°F [180°C].

In a small mixing bowl, whisk together the brown sugar, 3 Tbsp of the butter, 1 Tbsp of filtered water, and the corn syrup until well combined. Pour into an 8½ by 4½ in [21.5 by 11 cm] loaf pan. Set aside.

Place the remaining 5 Tbsp [70 g] of butter in another small bowl. In a third small bowl, mix the Jasmine Sugar and cinnamon with a spoon until combined.

Take one piece of the biscuit dough and dip it into the melted butter to completely coat all sides with a light coating. Then dip the biscuit into the Jasmine Sugar mixture and lightly coat all sides. Place the biscuit into the loaf pan on its thinner side atop the brown sugar mixture. Continue this process with each biscuit, setting each one in the pan on its side up against the next biscuit until the pan is full.

Place the pan in the oven and bake for 30 to 45 minutes until the biscuits in the center of the pan have cooked through and the tops are dark golden brown. Let cool for 5 minutes, then overturn the entire pan onto a pretty plate or tray. Serve immediately.

FLORAL DOUGHNUTS FOUR WAYS

3 ⅓ cups [465 g] all-purpose flour, plus more for dusting

¾ cup [180 ml] warm filtered water

¼ cup [50 g] granulated sugar (you can also use ¼ cup [40 g] Garden Party Sugar [page 19] if you're feeling festive)

4 tsp active dry yeast

2 tsp Rose Salt (page 15) or Chamomile Salt (page 14)

4 large eggs

9 Tbsp [130 g] unsalted butter, at room temperature

4 cups [960 ml] organic canola oil

1 batch icing of your choice (recipes follow)

Warm, chewy, and quite pretty, I may add, these Floral Doughnuts are an exquisite way to impress your family and start the weekend off with a well-deserved celebration. Making homemade doughnuts can sound a bit overwhelming, but once you get the process down, it's so much fun and is a great activity for the whole family to enjoy. We like to whip up a batch of these beauties and hand them out to our neighbors as a surprise treat.

MAKES APPROXIMATELY
2 DOZEN DOUGHNUTS

In the bowl of a stand mixer fitted with the dough hook, place the flour, water, sugar, yeast, Rose Salt, and eggs and mix on low speed for about 6 minutes until the dough begins to become elastic. Increase the speed to medium and add pieces of butter slowly, about 1 or 2 Tbsp at a time, until well combined, an additional 7 or 8 minutes. If needed, occasionally stop the mixer to scrape down the sides of the bowl. Cover the mixing bowl with plastic wrap or a kitchen towel and allow the dough to rise in a warm spot until it has about doubled in size, 1 or 2 hours.

Transfer the dough to a lightly floured surface. Dust a rolling pin with flour and roll the dough out to a thickness of about ¾ in [2 cm]. Using a 2½ in [6 cm] round cookie cutter dusted with flour and the large side of a round piping tip dusted with flour, cut out the doughnuts and centers. You can use the center pieces to make doughnut holes if you'd like, which will reduce the yield to about 20 doughnuts. Or you can combine the center pieces with the leftover dough scraps and roll it out again to make an additional 3 or 4 doughnuts. Transfer the doughnuts to two parchment-lined baking sheets and cover each with a kitchen towel. Allow the dough to rise for another hour.

Place a wire rack or paper towels in a parchment-lined baking sheet. Pour the oil into a Dutch-style oven or other large pot and bring the temperature up to 360°F [183°C]. The temperature can shift as you begin to fry the doughnuts, so be sure to keep an eye on the temperature and raise or lower the heat as needed. Place 2 doughnuts in the oil and cook for 1 to 2 minutes. Flip each doughnut once the underside turns golden in color and cook for 1 to 2 minutes more. Using a slotted spoon, transfer the doughnuts from the oil to the prepared baking sheet and let cool slightly. Once you have finished frying the doughnuts and they are cool enough to handle, dunk the tops of the doughnuts into the icing of your choice, turning the doughnuts as you dip. Place the doughnuts on a wire rack and garnish as directed in the icing recipe. Allow the icing to set for about 5 minutes, and then serve immediately.

CONTINUED

Strawberry Chamomile

2 tsp dried chamomile

2 cups [200 g] sifted confectioners' sugar, plus more as needed

3 Tbsp whole milk, plus more as needed

3 Tbsp fresh mashed strawberries

Fresh chamomile, for garnish (optional)

½ tsp Rose Salt (page 15), for garnish

FOR APPROXIMATELY 2 DOZEN DOUGHNUTS

Using a mortar and pestle or spice grinder, grind the dried chamomile until the blooms resemble small sprinkles. In a medium mixing bowl, whisk together the confectioners' sugar, milk, strawberries, and dried chamomile until combined. If the icing is a little soupy, add an additional 1 tsp of confectioners' sugar. If the icing is a little thick, add an additional 1 tsp of milk. When the doughnuts are ready to be iced, follow the icing instructions on page 61. Sprinkle with the fresh chamomile, if using, and the Rose Salt. After the icing sets, serve immediately.

Hibiscus Lemon Glaze with Fresh Edible Flowers

1½ tsp dried hibiscus

2 cups [200 g] sifted confectioners' sugar, plus more as needed

¼ cup [60 ml] whole milk, plus more as needed

1 tsp lemon zest

½ cup [10 to 12 g] fresh edible flowers (such as small pansies or violets), for garnish

FOR APPROXIMATELY 2 DOZEN DOUGHNUTS

Using a mortar and pestle or spice grinder, grind the hibiscus until the blooms resemble small flakes. In a medium mixing bowl, whisk together the confectioners' sugar, milk, lemon zest, and hibiscus until combined. If the icing is a little soupy, add an additional 1 tsp of confectioners' sugar. If the icing is a little thick, add an additional 1 tsp of milk. When the doughnuts are ready to be iced, follow the icing instructions on page 61. Gently press 2 or 3 fresh flowers into the icing of each doughnut. After the icing sets, serve immediately.

Rose-Salted Milk Chocolate

3 oz [85 g] high-quality milk hocolate (I like to use Scharffen Berger 41% milk chocolate)

¼ cup [55 g] Rose Butter (page 20)

2 Tbsp whole milk

1 tsp organic light corn syrup

1 tsp vanilla extract

1 cup [100 g] sifted confectioners' sugar

½ tsp Rose Salt (page 15), for garnish

FOR APPROXIMATELY 2 DOZEN DOUGHNUTS

In a medium saucepan over medium-low heat, melt the chocolate slowly, stirring constantly. Add the Rose Butter, milk, corn syrup, and vanilla. Continue stirring until the mixture is smooth. Remove from the heat and let cool slightly. Add the confectioners' sugar and whisk until completely blended. When the doughnuts are ready to be iced, follow the icing instructions on page 61. Sprinkle with the Rose Salt. Allow the icing to set for about 5 minutes. Serve immediately.

Boysenberry Jasmine

tsp fragrant jasmine tea leaves

2 cups [200 g] sifted confectioners' sugar, plus more as needed

3 Tbsp whole milk, plus more as needed

3 Tbsp fresh mashed boysenberries

FOR APPROXIMATELY 2 DOZEN DOUGHNUTS

Using a mortar and pestle or spice grinder, grind the jasmine until it resembles small flakes. In a medium mixing bowl, whisk together the confectioners' sugar, milk, boysenberries, and jasmine until combined. If the icing is a little soupy, add an additional 1 tsp of confectioners' sugar. If the icing is a little thick, add an additional 1 tsp of whole milk. When the doughnuts are ready to be iced, follow the icing instructions on page 61. After the icing sets, serve immediately.

CRUST

1⅓ cups [160 g] sifted
all-purpose flour

1 tsp Chamomile Salt (page 14)

½ cup [110 g] unsalted
butter, cut into small cubes

FILLING

4 large eggs

¾ cup [180 ml] half-and-half

¼ cup [60 ml] whole milk

2 Tbsp sour cream

½ tsp Chamomile Salt (page 14)

¼ cup [22 g] chopped
cooked crispy bacon

½ cup [40 g] grated Gouda

4 Tbsp [8 g] grated Parmigiano

4 Tbsp [10 g] chopped
blooming herbs (I used a
combination of rosemary,
oregano, marjoram,
and parsley)

2 Tbsp fresh calendula petals

EGG WASH

1 large egg

1 Tbsp heavy cream
or half-and-half

This delicious quiche puts on quite a show at the brunch or tea table. Vibrant, fresh calendula petals and blooming herbs add a pretty confetti to this savory treat . . . and paired with the saltiness of Gouda and bacon? It's absolutely lovely in every way.

SERVES 8

To make the crust: In a large mixing bowl, whisk together the flour and Chamomile Salt until combined. Add the butter and, using your hands, press it into the flour mixture until the dough resembles flakes. Add ¼ cup [60 ml] of filtered water and mix again with your hands until just combined. Form the dough into a small disk and wrap it in plastic wrap. Store in the refrigerator until ready to use, up to a week. If it's a hot day, I like to let the dough rest in the refrigerator for about an hour.

To make the filling: While the dough is resting in the refrigerator, start on the filling. In a large mixing bowl, whisk the eggs until the yolks blend with the whites. Add the half-and-half, whole milk, sour cream, Chamomile Salt, bacon, Gouda, 3 Tbsp of the Parmigiano, 3 Tbsp of the blooming herbs, and the calendula petals. Whisk together until just combined. Store in the refrigerator until ready to use.

CONTINUE

NOTE: I love serving this quiche with a floral side salad. Simply take ½ cup [20 g] of mixed greens per serving and add 3 Tbsp of fresh flower petals. Squeeze a quartered lemon over the top, drizzle with olive oil, and sprinkle with a pinch of Chamomile Salt (page 14). Voilà! A gorgeous floral side salad to accompany this beautiful quiche.

To make the quiche: Preheat the oven to 350°F [180°C]. Butter a 9 in [23 cm] ceramic tart dish. Set aside.

Lightly flour a large, clean work surface. Using a rolling pin, roll out the dough into a circle about 10 in [25 cm] in diameter. Transfer the dough to the tart dish and press it in gently. Using a fork, prick holes into the dough to allow steam to escape while baking; about 10 pricks will do.

Pour the quiche filling into the tart dish. Sprinkle with the remaining 1 Tbsp of Parmigiano.

To make the egg wash: In a small bowl, whisk together the egg and cream until well combined. Using a pastry brush, brush the egg wash on the exposed crust.

Bake the quiche for about 40 minutes until the filling has just set. Let cool for 15 minutes before serving. Sprinkle with the remaining 1 Tbsp of chopped herbs. Store leftovers in an airtight container in the refrigerator for up to 2 days.

COFFEE WITH GARDEN PARTY CREAMER

GARDEN PARTY CREAMER

½ cup [80 g] Garden Party Sugar (page 19)

¼ cup [60 ml] half-and-half

4 cups [960 ml] freshly brewed coffee

I love surprising guests with this floral coffee in the morning or even for a teatime treat. You can serve it elegantly on a tray or table and place the Garden Party Creamer in a pretty little pitcher. Allow guests to serve themselves or add about 2 Tbsp of creamer to each cup of coffee. And how fun is it to say Garden Party Creamer? Just about as fun as making this fragrant indulgence.

SERVES 4

To make the Garden Party Creamer: In a small saucepan over medium heat, stir together the Garden Party Sugar and ¼ cup [60 ml] of filtered water. Cook, stirring occasionally, until the sugar has completely dissolved and the mixture has thickened into a syrup, about 5 minutes. Remove from the heat and let cool for 5 minutes.

Strain the mixture through a fine-mesh sieve set over a small bowl. Allow the syrup to cool completely, 15 to 20 minutes. Add the half-and-half and stir until combined.

Divide the coffee between four cups and serve with the creamer alongside.

GARDEN PARTY ICED COFFEE

Serve this beverage iced and you'll have yourself a delicious Garden Party Iced Coffee! Simply cool the coffee in the refrigerator overnight and pour into four ice-filled tumblers. Add the Garden Party Creamer as you please.

TIPS FOR GROWING EDIBLE FLOWERS AT HOME

Whether you want to start growing edible flowers in your house in a pot or two or outdoors in a small garden, these blooms are easy to grow, and it's so fun to always have them on hand! Overall, be sure to only grow organic edible flowers. Consult your local nursery for what grows best in your area. Some of my favorites? Lavender and chamomile are quite versatile and tend to require minimal maintenance, whether indoors or out. Nasturtium is also quite lovely, and if it grows well in your area, it can fill your garden with gorgeous blooms year-round.

HERE ARE A FEW TIPS AND HELPFUL STEPS FOR GROWING EDIBLE FLOWERS INSIDE

Don't be afraid to start small.

Ask your local garden center for a bag of high-quality potting soil.

Find pots that you think are pretty and fill them with potting soil.

Plant your pots with seeds from your favorite edibles and then set them in a sunny spot.

Follow the instructions on your pack of seeds.

Use a watering can to water your plants in the sink so the excess water can drain out.

Water often enough to keep the soil thoroughly moistened until sprouts appear, then water deeply (until water runs out of the bottom of the pot) and infrequently without letting the soil completely dry out.

Sit back and watch the magic happen.

Don't be afraid to be ambitious!

If you have the space, the desire, and the means, dig a garden bed—or two—and grow some flowers!

Obtain a sturdy spading fork. You may not even have to purchase one! Simply ask around and a friend may have one you can borrow.

Buy compost from your favorite nursery, or get some from a friend's amazing compost pile.

Use a spading fork to incorporate the compost into your soil by plunging the fork into the earth and turning over the soil.

Flip the spading fork and use its tines to break apart any larger chunks of soil.

Work the soil gently for as long as your muscles can stand.

You're done when you've achieved a pleasing crumb structure in the topsoil.

Use the fork to level the seedbed—you are now ready to plant seeds.

Follow the directions on the seed packets for planting and watering.

Have fun, take deep breaths, and enjoy a floral libation while you work!

See page 96 for sources on purchasing edible flower seeds.

CHAPTER 3

FLORAL

AFTERNOON TEA

A FLORAL CHEESE BOARD

CHEESES

2 or 3 hard cheeses (such as Gouda, Manchego, or Cheddar)

2 or 3 soft cheeses (such as Brie, blue cheese, or Camembert)

Borage Cream Cheese (page 88) and Floral Chèvre (page 86; optional, if you're feeling ambitious)

FROM THE FLORAL PANTRY

Floral Infused Honey (page 27)

Apricot Chamomile Jam (page 26)

FRUIT

2 to 3 cups [240 to 420 g] seasonal fruit (berries and sliced stone fruit in spring and summer, sliced persimmons, apples, and pears in fall and winter)

BAKED FLORAL GOODIES (RECIPES FOLLOW)

Cheddar Calendula Crackers

Rosy Rosemary Chamomile-Salted Roasted Cashews

There are few things better as a party guest than arriving to find a glorious cheese board set up for you to enjoy. This Floral Cheese Board will make your guests gasp with delight. It's absolutely stunning and full of so many homemade floral goodies to nibble on.

SERVES APPROXIMATELY 15 AS AN APPETIZER

Set out a large marble pastry board or an extra-large wooden cutting board. Lay out the cheeses first, arranging them evenly around the board. Spoon the honey and jam into little bowls, each with a small spoon or knife for serving, and place the bowls on the cheese board. I like to place the honey next to a soft cheese and the jam next to a hard cheese. Organize the fruit around the board by variety, then fan out crackers to fill any remaining spaces. You can pour the cashews directly onto the board or place them in a small bowl with a serving spoon if you'd like. Be sure to garnish your cheese board with lots of edible flowers, such as blooming herbs, nasturtium, pansies, chamomile, and even roses. Place a few cheese knives on your board for serving.

Cheddar Calendula Cracker

1½ cups [180 g] sifted all-purpose flour, plus more for dusting

2 cups [160 g] grated sharp Cheddar cheese

½ cup [110 g] unsalted butter, at room temperature (you can also use Rose Butter [page 20])

1 tsp Rose Salt (page 15)

2 Tbsp half-and-half

3 Tbsp fresh calendula petals

How I adore Martha Stewart. These crackers are a spin on her classic recipe, but I made a few floral additions to add some spice and color from fresh calendula petals and Rose Salt. These crackers are so rich and delicious and make a lovely addition to a gorgeous cheese board. I love nibbling on the leftovers with a warm bowl of homemade tomato soup.

MAKES APPROXIMATELY 20 CRACKERS

In a food processor, add the flour, Cheddar, butter, and Rose Salt. Pulse until the mixture resembles course crumbs. Add the half-and-half and mix until just combined. Sprinkle the calendula petals over the dough and remove the dough from the food processor, (you'll naturally press the flowers in a bit this way). Using your hands, shape the dough into a small, flat rectangle, then wrap the dough in plastic wrap or another wrap of your choice and place in the refrigerator for about 20 minutes.

Preheat the oven to 325°F [165°C]. Line two baking sheets with parchment paper.

Lightly flour a work surface and, using a rolling pin, roll out the dough to a thickness of about ¼ in [6 mm]. Using a 2½ in [6 cm] round cookie cutter, cut out crackers and place them on the prepared baking sheets. Reroll any remaining dough scraps and cut out more crackers. You can reroll the dough twice, but no more.

Bake the crackers for 25 to 30 minutes until the edges turn golden brown.

Transfer the crackers immediately to a wire rack to cool completely, and serve them that day—although you can store the leftovers at room temperature in an airtight container and nibble on them for up to 2 days.

Rosy Rosemary Chamomile-Salted Roasted Cashews

2 Tbsp Rose Butter (page 20)

1¼ cups [175 g] raw cashews

½ tsp Chamomile Salt (page 14)

½ tsp dried chamomile, chopped

1 tsp fresh rosemary, chopped

½ tsp dried rose petals, chopped

These roasted cashews are a great snack to have on hand and make a scrumptious addition to a cheese board. They also taste delicious chopped up and tossed into salads or as a garnish for a squash soup. There's nothing better than freshly roasted cashews in butter, especially when seasoned with florals and herbs.

MAKES APPROXIMATELY 8 OZ [225 G]

In a medium saucepan over medium heat, melt the Rose Butter. Add the cashews and after 1 minute, lower the heat to medium-low. Allow the cashews to slowly roast, stirring with a wooden spoon every minute or so. Keep a close eye on them so they don't brown too quickly, and adjust the heat as needed. Once the cashews are golden brown, season with the Chamomile Salt, dried chamomile, rosemary, and rose petals and mix with the wooden spoon. Remove from the heat and let cool for about 10 minutes before adding to your cheeseboard. Or allow to cool completely and store in an airtight container for up to 2 weeks.

BERRIES WITH LAVENDER WHIPPED CREAM

1 cup [240 ml] heavy whipping cream

3 Tbsp confectioners' sugar

1 tsp freshly ground dried lavender

4 cups [480 g] mixed berries (I love using raspberries, blackberries, blueberries, and boysenberries)

6 sprigs fresh lavender, for garnish

This elegant yet simple treat is so fresh and light. It's the perfect middle-of-summer delight when you are craving something sweet and refreshing. I love making a batch after we return from picking berries, when the fruit is as fresh and wild tasting as can be. Serve with a glass of Champagne with a Rose-Salted Rim (page 95) for a tasty treat.

SERVES 6

Using a stand mixer fitted with the whisk attachment, whip the cream on medium speed. Slowly add the confectioners' sugar and dried lavender. Whip for 1 or 2 minutes until soft peaks form, stopping to check the consistency as needed. You don't want it to get too chunky or thick, so keep an eye on it. Store, covered, in the refrigerator for up to 2 days.

Divide the berries between six small bowls, then spoon the lavender whipped cream atop each bowl of berries. Garnish each one with a sprig of lavender and serve.

1 cup [200 g] granulated sugar

½ cup [110 g] coconut oil, melted and cooled

2 large eggs

8 oz [230 g] canned pumpkin or fresh pumpkin purée

1 Tbsp orange blossom water

1½ cups [180 g] sifted all-purpose flour

3 Tbsp dried chamomile

1 tsp baking soda

½ tsp ground cinnamon

½ tsp freshly ground nutmeg

½ tsp Rose Salt (page 15)

¼ cup [45 g] chopped bittersweet chocolate

Unsalted butter, for greasing the pan

2 Tbsp confectioners' sugar, for garnish

Rose Butter or Floral Butter (page 20), for serving

This bread is splendid to bake anytime of year but I especially love to make it in autumn when the weather starts to turn a bit chilly and the farmers' markets are overflowing with pumpkins. Chamomile and orange blossom are beautiful additions to a traditional cinnamon-and-nutmeg-spiced pumpkin bread. The addition of bittersweet chocolate makes this pumpkin bread a wonderful teatime treat.

SERVES 8 TO 10

Preheat the oven to 350°F [180°C].

In the bowl of a stand mixer fitted with the paddle attachment, add the granulated sugar and oil. Mix on medium speed until well combined. Slowly add the eggs and mix until well combined. Add the pumpkin purée, ¼ cup plus 2 Tbsp [90 ml] of filtered water, and the orange blossom water and mix on medium speed until well combined.

In a medium mixing bowl, whisk together the flour, chamomile, baking soda, cinnamon, nutmeg, and Rose Salt. Slowly add the dry ingredients to the wet ingredients while mixing on low speed, then increase the speed to medium. Mix until well combined. Using a rubber spatula, fold in the chocolate.

Butter an 8½ by 4½ in [21.5 by 11 cm] loaf pan. Pour the batter into the loaf pan, then bake for approximately 50 minutes or until a toothpick inserted into the center comes out clean. You may need to cover the pan with aluminum foil halfway through baking if the top of the bread is browning too quickly.

Allow the bread to cool in the pan for 10 minutes, then remove it from the pan and transfer it onto a wire rack to let cool for an additional 10 minutes before serving. Using a small fine-mesh sieve, sprinkle the top of the bread with confectioner's sugar.

Once completely cooled, store the loaf in an airtight container at room temperature for 2 days.

Serve with Rose Butter or your favorite Floral Butter.

FLORAL TOASTS FOUR WAYS

Edible flowers are given a chance to show off their gorgeous petals and elegant flavors in these colorful, lively toasts. Each recipe makes one toast, so you can build one just for yourself or easily scale up depending on the number of people you're feeding.

Rose Geranium + Strawberry Jam with Mascarpone

2 Tbsp mascarpone

1 slice sourdough bread, toasted

2 Tbsp Rose Geranium and Strawberry Jam (page 23)

Fresh rose geranium, for garnish

Using a spreader knife or butter knife, evenly distribute the mascarpone on the toast. Using a spoon, gently spread the Rose Geranium and Strawberry Jam on top of the mascarpone, leaving a ⅜ in [1 cm] border so some of the mascarpone still shows around the edges. Garnish with fresh rose geranium.

Almond Butter with Chamomile Salt + Floral Infused Honey

2 Tbsp almond butter

1 slice sourdough bread, toasted

1½ tsp Floral Infused Honey (page 27)

¼ tsp Chamomile Salt (page 14)

Fresh chamomile, for garnish

Using a spreader knife or butter knife, evenly spread the almond butter on the toast. Drizzle the Floral Infused Honey on top and sprinkle with the Chamomile Salt. Garnish with chamomile flowers.

Apricot Chamomile Jam with Ricotta + Chopped Pistachios

2 Tbsp whole milk ricotta

1 slice rye bread, toasted

2 Tbsp Apricot Chamomile Jam (page 26)

1 Tbsp roasted and salted pistachios, chopped

Using a spreader knife or butter knife, evenly distribute the ricotta on the rye toast. Using a spoon, gently spread the Apricot Chamomile Jam on top of the ricotta, leaving a ⅜ in [1 cm] border so some of the ricotta still shows around the edges. Sprinkle with the pistachios.

Orange Blossom Chocolate Hazelnut Toast with Rose Petals

3 Tbsp Orange Blossom Chocolate Hazelnut Spread (page 28)

1 slice brioche, lightly toasted

1 Tbsp fresh edible rose petals

Pinch Rose Salt (page 15)

Using a spreader knife or butter knife, evenly distribute the Orange Blossom Chocolate Hazelnut Spread on the toast. Sprinkle with the rose petals and Rose Salt.

FLORAL CHÈVRE + CHAMOMILE-SALTED CUCUMBER TEA SANDWICHES

5 oz [140 g] chèvre

2 Tbsp fresh, edible flower petals, plus more for garnish (I like to use fresh lavender petals, rose geranium flowers, nasturtium, and small rose petals)

2 slices spongy white bread

12 very thinly cut peeled cucumber slices

⅛ tsp Chamomile Salt (page 14)

I love using a spongy white bread for these tea sandwiches in particular. It's a great contrast to the crunchy cucumber and is a lovely backdrop on which to display the colorful petals in the floral chèvre. This recipe is a base for four small tea sandwiches made with two slices of bread, so make multiple batches according to the number of guests you're expecting. Serve on pretty, tiered cake stands.

MAKES 4 SMALL
TEA SANDWICHES

Place about 1 oz [30 g] of the chèvre into a small mixing bowl. Sprinkle a pinch of the edible flowers on top. Add an additional 1 oz [30 g] of the chèvre and sprinkle with another pinch of the edible flowers. Continue this process until all of the chèvre and flower petals are in the mixing bowl. Place a small piece of plastic wrap on a clean counter or table. Using a rubber spatula, transfer the Floral Chèvre to the plastic wrap. Wrap and gently press the petals into the chèvre, forming a cylindrical shape. If not using immediately, store in the refrigerator and remove 30 minutes before use; it spreads best at room temperature.

Using a spreader knife or butter knife, spread 1½ Tbsp of the Floral Chèvre onto each slice of bread. Layer the slices of cucumber onto one of the pieces of bread and sprinkle with the Chamomile Salt. Gently press the two pieces of bread together to secure the cucumber slices. Using a sharp knife, slice off the crusts, then cut the sandwich into four equal pieces. Spread a little additional Floral Chèvre on the sides of the sandwiches and press some fresh petals into the sides for garnish. Serve the sandwiches on a platter.

Store any leftover Floral Chèvre, wrapped, in the refrigerator and use within a few days.

WATERMELON RADISH, SPRING PEA + BORAGE CREAM CHEESE TEA SANDWICHES

¼ cup [60 g] cream cheese, at room temperature

1 Tbsp fresh borage petals

8 baguette slices, about ¼ in [6 mm] thick

12 thinly cut watermelon radish slices

2 Tbsp fresh shelled spring peas

These tea sandwiches are crisp, light, and charmingly colorful. I like to use thin slices of baguette to make these sandwiches, but feel free to use your favorite loaf. If you would like to add a little more protein to these sandwiches, a touch of rotisserie chicken is always a delicious addition. This recipe is a base for four small tea sandwiches, so make multiple batches according to the number of guests you're expecting. Serve alongside Floral Chèvre and Chamomile-Salted Cucumber Tea Sandwiches (page 86).

MAKES 4 SMALL
TEA SANDWICHES

Place the cream cheese in a medium mixing bowl and sprinkle the borage petals on top. Place a small piece of plastic wrap on a clean counter or table. Using a rubber spatula, transfer the Borage Cream Cheese to the plastic wrap. Wrap and gently press the petals into the cream cheese, forming a cylindrical shape. If not using immediately, store in the refrigerator and remove 30 minutes before use; it spreads best at room temperature.

Lay out all of the baguette slices on a clean work surface. Add about ½ Tbsp of the Borage Cream Cheese to each slice of baguette. Add 3 slices of the watermelon radish each to 4 of the baguette slices, then sprinkle with the spring peas. Place the 4 remaining baguette slices on top of the radish–pea slices. Serve the sandwiches on a platter.

Store any leftover Borage Cream Cheese, wrapped, in the refrigerator and use within a few days.

RASPBERRY ELDERFLOWER SCONES

2 cups plus 3 Tbsp [310 g] all-purpose flour, plus more for rolling out the dough

¼ cup [50 g] granulated sugar or Garden Party Sugar [40 g] (page 19), plus more for sprinkling

1 tsp baking powder

¼ tsp baking soda

¼ tsp Rose Salt (page 15)

½ cup [110 g] unsalted butter, cut into small cubes

1 cup [240 ml] heavy whipping cream

¼ cup [60 ml] elderflower liqueur (such as St. Germain)

1 cup [120 g] fresh raspberries

These scones are wonderfully crisp on the outside and have a delectably soft texture on the inside. With a hint of elderflower sweetness and a burst of tartness from the raspberries, these morning delights pair beautifully with a piping hot cappuccino and a good magazine. I love preparing these scones the night before I bake so I can place them in the oven as soon as I wake up.

MAKES 8 LARGE SCONES

Preheat the oven to 400°F [200°C].

In a large mixing bowl, whisk together the flour, sugar, baking powder, baking soda, and Rose Salt. Add the butter to the mixture and, using your hands, combine until it resembles small flakes. Create a pool in the center of the mixture and add the heavy cream and elderflower liqueur. Using a rubber spatula, fold the flour mixture into the cream mixture. Once the dough comes together, gently fold in the berries. If the dough is too sticky and wet to handle, add more flour, 1 tsp at a time; this may depend on how juicy your raspberries are.

CONTINUED

Lightly flour a rolling pin and a cool work surface, such as a cutting board or marble pastry board, and transfer the dough to the work surface. Roll out the dough into about a 9 in [23 cm] round. Using a sharp knife dusted with flour, cut the dough into 8 large triangles. You can bake them immediately, or refrigerate them overnight before baking by placing them on a parchment-lined baking sheet and lightly covering them with plastic wrap. You can also freeze the dough at this stage and store it in the freezer in an airtight container for up to 1 month.

When you're ready to bake, line a baking sheet with parchment paper. Place the scones about 1 in [2.5 cm] apart on the sheet and sprinkle with more sugar. Bake for about 20 minutes or until golden brown (this may take a bit longer if baking from the refrigerator or freezer). Transfer the scones to a wire rack to cool for about 10 minutes before serving.

Be sure the scones are completely cool before transferring to an airtight container to store at room temperature for up to 2 days.

ROSE GERANIUM GIN DAISY COCKTAIL

4 oz [120 ml] gin

4 oz [120 ml] freshly squeezed lemon juice

2 Tbsp grenadine

2 Tbsp Rose Geranium Syrup (page 22)

Ice cubes

Fresh rose geranium, for garnish

This enchanting pink cocktail is a perfect addition to any afternoon high tea spread. Its gorgeous flavor and beautiful color will charm any guests at your fabulous soirée. Serve in pretty coupe glasses and garnish each with a rose geranium flower. Cheers!

MAKES 2 COCKTAILS

In a large cocktail shaker, combine the gin, lemon juice, grenadine, Rose Geranium Syrup, and ice. Shake vigorously for about 30 seconds. Strain into two coupe glasses, and garnish each glass with a rose geranium flower before serving.

3 Tbsp Rose Salt (page 15)

Lemon wedge

**1 bottle [750 ml] Champagne
or sparkling wine**

This charming libation is absolutely stunning. It gives Rose Salt a chance to shine in all of her glory. Simply rim a coupe glass or Champagne flute with a dusting of pretty Rose Salt and your glass of Champagne will be sparkling with even more effervescence at your next celebratory toast.

MAKES 4 COCKTAILS

MAKE IT
A FLORAL
CHAMPAGNE
COCKTAIL

Turn this libation into a Champagne cocktail by adding 1 Tbsp of Lavender Syrup (page 21) or Rose Geranium Syrup (page 22) to each glass before adding the Champagne.

Pour the Rose Salt into a shallow plate or bowl. Wet the rim of four coupe glasses or Champagne flutes with the lemon wedge and dip the rim in the Rose Salt, gently rolling it to coat. I typically prefer to only rim about half of the glass.

Pour about 6 oz [180 ml] of Champagne into each glass. Serve immediately!

SOURCING EDIBLE FLOWERS

There are three ways to get your hands on gorgeous and delicious edible blooms: Grow your own, buy them locally, or buy them online. If you're looking to purchase what you need, here are some tips on where and how you can shop for edible blooms.

SHOP LOCALLY FOR EDIBLE FLOWERS

A great first step is to check out the stores around you to look for edible flowers, both fresh and dried. The best place to find edible flowers is at natural and gourmet food stores, including national chains like Whole Foods and Sprouts. Look in the tea and bulk spices section for edible dried flowers. Orange blossom water and rose water can typically be found in the baking or international food aisles. Many natural food stores carry dried roses, lavender petals, chamomile, hibiscus, and calendula, just to name a few.

Packaged whole flower teas are another great way to find flowers to use for the recipes in this book. Just be sure to double-check the ingredients list, as sometimes the flowers are blended with black or green tea. It is of course completely okay to use teas in recipes as well—just be sure you know exactly what you are buying before using it in a recipe so you don't end up with an unexpected result. I like to use jasmine tea in recipes; for example, see Jasmine Sugar (page 18) and Boysenberry Jasmine Floral Doughnuts (page 65).

I'm usually able to find chamomile in its pure form (and not blended into a tea) in tea packets near the coffee/tea aisles. Natural or gourmet food stores may also carry fresh edible flowers during the holidays and spring and summer months as well. Don't see fresh edible flowers at your local grocery store? Talk to the produce manager about the possibility of getting them in stock.

If your town has a farmers' market, take a stroll through it and you may find fresh edible flowers. You can also look for flowering herbs, such as rosemary, thyme, sage, and rose geranium (see page 141).

DRIED VERSUS FRESH FLOWERS

Dried flowers are a lot easier to find than fresh flowers. They are also much easier to use in recipes because they tend to stand up to cooking a lot better than fresh flowers and generally have a richer flavor. They also have a longer shelf life: You can store edible dried flowers in an airtight container for up to 6 months. Most of the recipes in this book call for dried flowers for these reasons.

But fresh flowers have plenty of lovely uses too. Fresh flowers are great to use for garnishes, such as on top of doughnuts (see page 60). Sprinkle in your favorite batters, doughs, and even salads (see page 16 for more tips). When you purchase fresh flowers, simply brush them off or wipe with a damp cloth before using. If you rinse them with water, the petals may wilt and lose some of their vibrancy. Use fresh edible flowers within a few days of purchasing.

SHOP FOR EDIBLE FLOWERS ONLINE

Edible flowers are increasing in popularity, and with new flower vendors popping up all the time, a simple online search can be a rewarding endeavor. But for a more targeted search, these are my favorite sources.

Etsy: Simply search for edible flowers on Etsy; there are many shops listed. Anything from dried dandelion flowers to lavender petals can be found on this useful sourcing site. Many shops offer prepackaged flowers, and others sell in bulk so you can order a specified weight. (www.etsy.com)

Terrain: You can find a variety of edible flowers on the Terrain website in addition to in its stores. It also sells a fun edible-flower seed bomb if you would like to start your own garden at home. For more on growing your own blooms, see page 36. (www.shopterrain.com)

ALWAYS BUY ORGANIC FLOWERS

This is the number-one rule of using edible flowers. Conventional flowers may have dangerous pesticides, fungicides, or other chemical residues and should be avoided.

FLORAL

CHAPTER 4

DESSERTS

CHOCOLATE CHIP COOKIES WITH ROSE SALT

1 cup [120 g] sifted
all-purpose flour

½ tsp baking soda

¼ tsp Rose Salt (page 15),
plus more for sprinkling

¾ cup plus 1 Tbsp [180 g]
packed dark brown sugar

½ cup [110 g] unsalted
butter, melted and cooled

½ tsp almond extract

1 large egg

¾ cup [135 g] dark chocolate
chips or disks (I like to use
TCHO's baking chocolate disks)

This recipe is a perfect example of how adding a touch of floral flavor to a classic treat can bring a bit of fanciness and pizazz. I love the way these cookies look when served with the rose petal flakes from the Rose Salt sprinkled on top.

MAKES 12 COOKIES

Preheat the oven to 375°F [190°C]. Line a baking sheet with parchment paper. Set aside.

In a medium mixing bowl, whisk together the flour, baking soda, and Rose Salt until combined. In a large mixing bowl, use a whisk to beat the brown sugar, butter, and almond extract until creamy. Add the egg and continue to mix until well combined, about 2 minutes. Slowly add the flour mixture to the butter mixture and mix until smooth. Using a rubber spatula, gently fold in the chocolate chips.

Drop 2½ Tbsp–size rounds of cookie dough onto the prepared baking sheet. Sprinkle each with a dash of Rose Salt. Bake for about 9 minutes or until the edges are golden brown. Let cool for 2 minutes before using a metal spatula to transfer the cookies to a wire rack, and let cool for another 4 or 5 minutes before serving. Store any leftovers in an airtight container for up to 2 days.

STRAWBERRY SHORTCAKE WITH CHAMOMILE WHIPPED CREAM

STRAWBERRY SCONES

1 cup [120 g] sifted all-purpose flour, plus more for dusting

3 Tbsp granulated sugar, plus more for sprinkling

2 tsp baking powder

½ tsp Chamomile Salt (page 14)

2 Tbsp unsalted butter

1 Tbsp coconut oil (unflavored)

⅓ cup [80 ml] heavy whipping cream

1 large egg, beaten

¼ cup [35 g] sliced strawberries

WHIPPED CREAM

½ cup [120 ml] heavy whipping cream

3 Tbsp confectioners' sugar

1 tsp freshly ground dried chamomile

SYRUP

½ cup [170 g] Floral Infused Honey (page 27)

½ cup [70 g] sliced strawberries

This is my ode to the strawberry and her favorite floral friend, chamomile. In late spring and early summer when the strawberries are bursting, I love to make this layered treat filled with strawberry goodness in every bite—with chamomile thrown in for good measure. I also love serving the syrup atop Rose Geranium Ice Cream (page 124).

SERVES 6

To make the Strawberry Scones: Preheat the oven to 375°F [190°C]. Line a baking sheet with parchment paper. Set aside.

In a large mixing bowl, combine the flour, granulated sugar, baking powder, and Chamomile Salt. Add the butter and coconut oil and, using your hands, mix together until the dough resembles small flakes.

In a separate small bowl, combine the cream and half of the beaten egg. Add the cream mixture to the dry ingredients and mix together with a rubber spatula until just combined. Add the strawberries and fold in with the spatula until just combined. The dough should be moist yet workable. If you find it is too sticky, continue adding more flour (just 1 tsp at a time) until it reaches a workable consistency.

CONTINUE

1 cup [140 g] sliced strawberries

Small strawberries, left whole, for garnish

Fresh chamomile, for garnish

Turn the dough out onto a heavily floured surface. Using a rolling pin or your hands, roll out the dough to a thickness of about ¾ in [2 cm] and cut out rounds using a 2½ in [6 cm] round cutter. Using a pastry brush, brush the scones with the remaining half of the beaten egg. Sprinkle each scone with a pinch of granulated sugar.

Transfer the scones to the prepared baking sheet and bake for 15 to 18 minutes or until golden brown. Transfer to a wire rack. Let cool slightly before assembling your shortcakes.

To make the whipped cream: Using a stand mixer fitted with the whisk attachment, whip the cream on medium-low speed. Add the confectioners' sugar and chamomile. Whip for about 2 minutes on medium speed until stiff peaks form, stopping to check the consistency as needed. You don't want it to get too chunky or thick, so keep an eye on it. Store, covered, in the refrigerator for up to 2 days.

To make the syrup: In a medium saucepan over medium heat, combine 1 cup [240 ml] of filtered water, the Floral Infused Honey, and strawberries and simmer until the mixture begins to thicken into a syrup, 10 to 15 minutes, stirring occasionally with a wooden spoon. Lower the heat if the mixture begins to splatter. Remove from the heat and let cool for 10 minutes before serving. You can store the syrup in an airtight container in the refrigerator for up to 1 week and reheat as needed.

Cut each scone in half. Layer whipped cream between the scone halves and place some of the fresh sliced strawberries inside the scones. Sandwich the two scone halves together and drizzle each shortcake with syrup. Top with a whole strawberry and garnish with fresh chamomile flowers. Serve immediately with any remaining sliced strawberries.

Store leftover whipped cream, syrup, and strawberries in separate airtight containers in the refrigerator for up to 3 days. The scones should be stored at room temperature in an airtight container and can be kept for up to 3 days, but they are best enjoyed the day they're made.

CHOCOLATE CUPCAKES WITH ROSE BUTTER-CREAM FROSTING

CHOCOLATE CUPCAKES

2 cups [240 g] sifted all-purpose flour

⅔ cup [50 g] Dutch-processed cocoa

1¼ cups [250 g] packed dark brown sugar

½ cup [90 g] bittersweet chocolate chips or chopped bittersweet chocolate

½ cup [90 g] dark chocolate chips or chopped dark chocolate

1 tsp baking powder

1 tsp baking soda

1 tsp espresso powder or finely ground coffee

¾ tsp Rose Salt (page 15)

2 large eggs, beaten

¾ cup [180 ml] whole milk

½ cup [120 ml] coconut oil, melted and cooled

2 tsp vanilla extract

2 tsp Champagne vinegar

The fudgiest chocolate cupcake topped with a delicate rose buttercream frosting . . . such an elegant dessert to serve at any occasion. Whether it's a birthday party for a friend or a little one, a bridal shower, or a baby shower, these gorgeous cupcakes will bring a smile to your guests' faces and make their taste buds sing with delight. Top each one with a petite rose for a splendid effect.

MAKES APPROXIMATELY 16 CUPCAKES

To make the cupcakes: Preheat the oven to 350°F [180°C] and line muffin tins with your favorite cupcake liners. Set aside.

In a large mixing bowl, whisk together the flour, cocoa, brown sugar, bittersweet and dark chocolate chips, baking powder, baking soda, espresso powder, and Rose Salt until combined.

In a separate medium bowl, whisk together the eggs, milk, oil, vanilla, and vinegar until combined. Add the wet ingredients to the dry ingredients and mix with a wooden spoon until *just* combined.

CONTINUED

ROSE BUTTERCREAM FROSTING

2¼ cups [225 g] sifted confectioners' sugar

1 cup [220 g] unsalted butter, at room temperature

2 Tbsp whole milk

2 tsp dried rose petals

¼ tsp rose water

Petite fresh garden roses, for garnish (optional)

Fill the cupcake liners about three-quarters of the way full. Bake for 15 to 18 minutes or until a toothpick inserted in the center of a cupcake comes out clean. Allow the cupcakes to cool in the pan for just 2 to 3 minutes, then transfer to a wire rack. Let cool completely before frosting.

To make the frosting: In the bowl of a stand mixer fitted with the paddle attachment, beat the confectioners' sugar, butter, milk, rose petals, and rose water on low speed until combined. Increase the speed to medium to allow the frosting to whip slightly, about 2 minutes.

Once the cupcakes have cooled, frost each one using an offset spatula. Garnish with a petite garden rose, if desired. Serve on a tiered cake stand or pretty tray.

Store leftovers in an airtight container at room temperature for up to 2 days.

JASMINE FLOURLESS CHOCOLATE CAKE

¾ cup [135 g] chopped bittersweet chocolate

¼ cup [55 g] unsalted butter, plus more for greasing

3 large eggs, yolks and whites separated

¼ cup [55 g] Jasmine Sugar (page 18)

½ tsp Rose Salt (page 15)

½ tsp vanilla extract

Confectioners' sugar, for garnish

Fresh jasmine blooms, for garnish (optional)

When you are in the mood for chocolatey goodness, there's nothing like whipping up a flourless chocolate cake to indulge in. With the addition of aromatic jasmine, this cake turns into an exotic treat.

MAKES ONE 9 IN [23 CM] CAKE

Preheat the oven to 350°F [180°C]. Butter a 9 in [23 cm] tart pan with a removable base and set aside.

In a double boiler (you can create one by placing a large, heatproof mixing bowl over a large saucepan filled with 2 in [5 cm] of water) over medium-low heat, add the chocolate, butter, egg yolks, Jasmine Sugar, Rose Salt, and vanilla. Allow the butter and chocolate to melt and stir constantly until the mixture is well combined and glossy.

Place the egg whites in a large mixing bowl and, using a whisk or handheld mixer fitted with the whisk attachment, beat until the egg whites start to form soft peaks. Pour the chocolate mixture into the egg whites and use a rubber spatula to fold it in until just combined. Pour the batter into the prepared tart pan.

CONTINUED

TIP: Serve this cake with a Jasmine Whipped Cream. Use my recipe for Lavender Whipped Cream (page 79) and simply swap out the lavender for jasmine tea.

Bake for 10 to 15 minutes until the cake has just set and a toothpick inserted into the center comes out clean. Let cool for 5 minutes. Transfer the tart pan to a wire rack and let cool for an additional 5 to 10 minutes.

Using a small fine-mesh sieve, sprinkle the top of the cake with confectioners' sugar. Scatter the jasmine over the cake if using. Serve immediately. Store leftovers in an airtight container at room temperature and enjoy within 2 days.

GARDEN PARTY LAYER CAKE WITH STRAWBERRY HIBISCUS JAM FROSTING

GARDEN PARTY CAKE

1 cup [220 g] unsalted butter, at room temperature, plus more for greasing the pans

1½ cups [250 g] Garden Party Sugar (page 19)

1 tsp Rose Salt (page 15)

1 tsp orange blossom water

¼ tsp rose water

6 large egg whites, at room temperature

1½ cups [360 ml] whole milk, at room temperature

3½ cups [420 g] cake flour

4 tsp baking powder

This cake is so pretty and elegant. Filled with so many floral ingredients, it certainly lives up to its name. From rose water to orange blossom water and floral-infused sugar filled with lavender, hibiscus, chamomile, and calendula, this luscious cake will make you feel like you are dining in the middle of a glorious garden, celebrating flowers in all of their splendor. And to top it off? This cake is decorated with a pretty-in-pink frosting, making it the loveliest pastry you ever did see. Be sure to top your cake with gorgeous blooms and a few petite strawberries.

MAKES A 9 IN [23 CM] TWO-LAYER CAKE

To make the cake: Preheat the oven to 350°F [180°C]. Butter two 9 in [23 cm] cake pans and cut out two pieces of parchment paper to fit the bottom of each pan. Lightly butter the parchment paper. Set aside.

In the bowl of a stand mixer fitted with the paddle attachment, beat the butter, Garden Party Sugar, and Rose Salt on medium speed until well combined. Add the orange blossom water and rose water and mix on medium speed until combined.

CONTINUED

STRAWBERRY HIBISCUS JAM FROSTING

¾ cup [105 g] chopped strawberries

2 Tbsp granulated sugar

1 Tbsp freshly squeezed lemon juice

½ tsp dried hibiscus petals

1 cup [220 g] unsalted butter, at room temperature

3½ cups [350 g] sifted confectioners' sugar

2 tsp half-and-half

Handful of edible blooms, for garnish

Petite strawberries, for garnish

TIP: You can easily double the amount of jam you make and then enjoy it spread on toast or drizzled on top of chocolate ice cream. Store it in an airtight container in the refrigerator for up to 3 weeks.

In a small mixing bowl with a spout, whisk together the egg whites and milk until well blended. Set aside.

In a separate medium mixing bowl, whisk together the cake flour and baking powder until just combined. Add about half of the egg white mixture to the bowl of the stand mixer and mix on low speed for about 30 seconds. Then add half of the flour mixture to the bowl of the stand mixer and mix on low speed for about 30 seconds. Repeat this process, then mix the batter on medium speed until it just comes together, scraping down the sides of the bowl with a rubber spatula as needed.

Divide the cake batter between the two cake pans and bake for 25 minutes or until a toothpick inserted into the center comes out clean. Allow the cakes to cool for a few minutes in the pans before transferring them to a wire rack to cool completely before frosting.

To make the frosting: In a medium saucepan over medium heat, mix together the strawberries, ¼ cup [60 ml] of filtered water, the granulated sugar, lemon juice, and hibiscus with a wooden spoon until combined. Bring the mixture to a simmer and lower the heat as needed if it starts to boil. Simmer for 20 to 30 minutes until it thickens and turns glossy.

Transfer the jam to a heatproof bowl or jar and let cool on the counter for about 1 hour before using. The jam will continue to thicken as it cools.

CONTINUE▶

Place the butter in the bowl of a stand mixer fitted with the paddle attachment. Mix on high speed for about 1 minute. Add the confectioners' sugar and begin to mix on low speed, slowly adding the half-and-half. Whip the frosting on high speed for about 1 minute until fluffy. Using a rubber spatula, fold in ¼ cup [75 g] of the jam until well combined.

Set one of the cakes on a serving platter or cake stand, and spread about one-quarter of the frosting on top. Place the second cake on top of the first and spread about half of the frosting on top. Spread the remaining quarter of the frosting around the sides of the two layers. Garnish with fresh flowers and strawberries and serve. This cake is best enjoyed the day it is frosted, but it can be stored in a cool space for up to 24 hours.

GARDEN PARTY STONE FRUIT GALETTE

CRUST

1⅓ cups [160 g] sifted
all-purpose flour, plus
more for dusting

1 tsp Chamomile Salt (page 14)

½ cup [110 g] unsalted
butter, cut into small cubes

1 tsp Garden Party Sugar
(page 19), for sprinkling

FILLING

3½ cups [585 g]
sliced stone fruit

¼ cup [40 g] Garden
Party Sugar (page 19)

3 Tbsp cornstarch, plus
more as needed

1 tsp freshly squeezed lemon
juice, plus more as needed

EGG WASH

1 large egg

1 Tbsp heavy cream

1 Tbsp Rose Geranium and
Strawberry Jam (page 23)

Fresh chamomile, for
garnish (optional)

When stone fruit season is peaking and my kitchen table is covered with fresh peaches, nectarines, and pluots, I love making this wonderfully fragrant and beautiful galette. The sides of the crust are sprinkled with Garden Party Sugar, adding a touch of nature's confetti to an already scrumptious treat. Serve with your favorite vanilla ice cream or make a batch of Rose Geranium Ice Cream (page 124) to accompany this delectable goodie.

SERVES 8

To make the crust: In a large mixing bowl, whisk together the flour and Chamomile Salt until combined. Add the butter and, using your hands, press the butter into the flour mixture until the dough resembles flakes. Add ¼ cup [60 ml] of filtered water and mix with your hands until just combined. Form the dough into a small disk and wrap it in plastic wrap. Store in the refrigerator until ready to use. If it's a hot day, I like to let the dough rest in the refrigerator for about 1 hour.

To make the filling: In a large mixing bowl, gently mix together the fruit, Garden Party Sugar, cornstarch, and lemon juice with a rubber spatula until well combined. If the filling appears to be very juicy, you may need to add an additional 1 tsp of cornstarch. If the

CONTINUED

filling appears to be on the dry side, add another 1 tsp of lemon juice. Set aside.

To make the galette: Preheat the oven to 400°F [200°C]. Line a large baking sheet with parchment paper. Set aside.

Lightly flour a large, clean work surface and use a rolling pin to roll out the dough into about a 12 in [30.5 cm] circle. Transfer the dough to the prepared baking sheet. Leaving about a 1½ in [4 cm] border, place the filling on top of the dough and spread it out evenly. Fold the remaining border of the dough over the filling.

To make the egg wash: In a small bowl, whisk together the egg and cream until well combined. Using a pastry brush, brush the egg wash on the crust. Sprinkle the crust with the 1 tsp of Garden Party Sugar.

Place the baking sheet in the oven and bake until the crust is golden brown and the filling is bubbling, about 35 minutes. Once you remove the galette from the oven, use the pastry brush to brush the top of the fruit with the Rose Geranium and Strawberry Jam to make it nice and glossy.

Allow the galette to cool on a wire rack for at least 30 minutes before serving. Garnish with chamomile flowers, if desired.

If you happen to have any of this wonderful galette left over, store it, covered, at room temperature and consume within 2 days.

OLALLIEBERRY HIBISCUS PIE

PIE CRUST

2¾ cups [330 g] sifted all-purpose flour, plus more for dusting

1 tsp Chamomile Salt (page 14)

1 cup [220 g] cold unsalted butter, cut into small cubes

½ cup [120 ml] ice-cold filtered water

FILLING

6 cups [720 g] olallieberries

1 cup [200 g] granulated sugar

3 Tbsp dried hibiscus

3 Tbsp cornstarch

EGG WASH

1 large egg

1 Tbsp heavy whipping cream

Making this pie is one of my favorite things to do every summer. I wait in anticipation for the berry farm down the road to open up their u-pick for their amazing olallieberry harvest. And the addition of hibiscus to any berry pie is such a treat; the color alone is a knockout and the bloom adds a tanginess that's wonderful in every way. Feel free to use your favorite berry in this recipe—or even a combination of a few if you wish—and serve it with Rose Geranium Ice Cream (page 124) if you're feeling fancy.

MAKES ONE 9 IN [23 CM] PIE

To make the crust: In a food processor, pulse the flour and Chamomile Salt a few times. Add the butter and mix for another 10 seconds or until the dough resembles flakes. Add the water in a slow stream and blend until small beads of dough begin to form and the dough just starts to come together.

Transfer the dough to a lightly floured work surface, cut it in half, and use your hands to form the dough into two disks (but try to handle the dough as little as possible). Roll out both disks into circles about 10 in [25 cm] wide. Wrap the dough in plastic wrap and place in the refrigerator until ready to use.

CONTINUED

Preheat the oven to 375°F [190°C]. Butter a 9 in [23 cm] ceramic pie dish.

To make the filling: In a large mixing bowl, gently mix together the berries, sugar, hibiscus, and cornstarch with a rubber spatula until combined, then set aside.

Using your fingers, press one unwrapped dough round into the pie dish. Use a fork to prick holes into the dough to allow steam to escape while baking—about ten pricks will do. Using kitchen shears or a pizza cutter, cut the second round of dough into strips about 1 in [2.5 cm] wide. Don't be afraid to use a ruler for this step! It can really help guide the cut so you have even strips for your lattice top.

Pour the berry mixture into the pie dish. Place about five parallel strips of dough on top of the filling, leaving a slight space between each one so that the filling peeks through. Then, fold back every other strip and place a strip of dough perpendicular to the parallel strips. Lay the parallel strips back down over the perpendicular strip. Next, take the parallel strips running beneath the perpendicular strip and fold them back over the perpendicular strip. Lay down a second perpendicular strip, leaving some space between the two, and again lay the parallel strips back down on top of the perpendicular strip. Continue this process to complete the lattice weaving. Using your fingers or a fork, crimp the edges of the dough with the pieces of lattice to secure the dough strips. Trim the excess dough and continue to crimp the edges of the dough as desired.

To make the egg wash: In a small bowl, beat together the egg and cream until well combined. Using a pastry brush, brush the pie dough with the egg wash. Transfer the pie to a baking sheet and bake for 60 to 70 minutes until the crust turns golden brown and the filling is bubbling. Keep an eye on the pie, as you may want to cover it with a pie guard or foil tent if the crust browns quickly. Allow the pie to cool for at least 30 to 45 minutes before serving.

If you have any pie left over, wrap it lightly and store it at room temperature for up to 2 days. It makes a lovely breakfast with a hot cup of coffee.

LEMON + HIBISCUS ICE POPS

⅓ cup [65 g] granulated sugar

2 tsp dried hibiscus

1¼ cups [300 ml] freshly
squeezed lemon juice

20 to 30 fresh
chamomile flowers

6 ice pop sticks

The ideal mix of tangy and sweet, these ice pops make the perfect summertime treat. They taste like floral lemonade and are the prettiest shade of pink. Adorned with beautiful chamomile flowers, they're the perfect pick-me-up in the peak of the summer heat.

MAKES APPROXIMATELY
SIX 3 FL OZ [90 ML] ICE POPS

In a small saucepan over medium heat, combine 2½ Tbsp of filtered water, the sugar, and hibiscus. Allow the mixture to simmer gently, stirring occasionally until the sugar dissolves. Remove from the heat and let steep for about 5 minutes. Strain the syrup into a small bowl through a fine-mesh sieve and let cool to room temperature before using.

In a large mixing bowl with a pour spout, whisk together the cooled syrup, lemon juice, and ½ cup and 2 Tbsp [150 ml] of filtered water. Pour about half of the mixture into a 6-piece ice pop mold, filling each cup only half way. Place a few chamomile flowers in each ice pop, then place the whole mold in the freezer for about 30 minutes. Remove from the freezer and fill the cups with the remaining mix. Add a few more chamomile flowers in each cup, then add the ice pop sticks. Place the mold back in the freezer for about 3 hours. Remove 5 minutes prior to serving.

Keep the pops in their molds until ready to consume, storing in the freezer of course! These ice pops should keep for up to a week.

ROSE GERANIUM ICE CREAM

6 large egg yolks

1½ cups [360 ml] heavy whipping cream

1 cup [240 ml] half-and-half

½ cup [120 ml] whole milk

⅔ cup [130 g] granulated sugar

¼ tsp Rose Salt (page 15)

10 fresh medium-size rose geranium leaves

Fresh rose geranium blooms, for garnish

My love for rose geranium continues to grow the more I use it. Its rosy flavor is so elegant and sophisticated, and this recipe is a favorite of mine. It's so simple in the best way. Serve it on its own or use it to top a homemade pie (see page 118). You'll find yourself making this treat again and again and your heart will be oh-so-happy (and your belly will be too).

SERVES 6

In a medium mixing bowl, whisk together the egg yolks until just combined. Set aside.

In a large Dutch oven, add the whipping cream, half-and-half, milk, sugar, Rose Salt, and rose geranium leaves. Place over medium heat and allow the mixture to steam, stirring occasionally, until the sugar has dissolved. Be sure the mixture doesn't boil. Remove from the heat and allow the rose geranium leaves to steep for 5 minutes.

Using tongs or a spoon, remove the rose geranium leaves and discard. The mixture should still be very hot. Ladle about ½ cup [120 ml] of the mixture into the bowl with the egg yolks, whisking constantly until combined. Add the egg yolk mixture to the Dutch oven and place back over medium heat. Using a wooden spoon, stir the mixture constantly. Keep a close eye on the temperature and don't allow the mixture to boil, lowering the heat as needed. Once

TIP: For an extravagant treat, make a floral banana split! Grab a plate or bowl of your choice and layer Rose Geranium Ice Cream atop a bed of split fresh bananas. Add your favorite chocolate ice cream. Drizzle with Hibiscus Syrup (page 34) and top with chopped Rose-Salted Almonds (page 131) and, of course, a cherry. Sprinkle with Rose Salt (page 15) and rose geranium blooms, and voilà! A gorgeous, indulgent floral dessert that will have everyone licking their spoons.

the mixture thickens and coats the back of the wooden spoon (5 to 7 minutes), remove the Dutch oven from the heat.

Place a large fine-mesh sieve over a large glass storage container. Pour the mixture through the sieve into the storage container, using a rubber spatula to press the mixture through the sieve. Cover and store in the freezer for about 45 minutes.

Remove the mixture from the freezer and pour it into an ice cream machine. Churn the mixture according to the manufacturer's instructions. Transfer the ice cream to a covered glass storage container and freeze for at least 1 or 2 hours before serving.

Scoop the ice cream into your favorite ice cream cone or bowl. Sprinkle with rose geranium blooms. This ice cream keeps in an airtight container in the freezer for up to 2 weeks, but the flavor is best in the first week.

10 oz [280 g] high-quality vanilla ice cream

½ cup [120 ml] whole milk

¼ cup [75 g] Rose Geranium and Strawberry Jam (page 23)

Fresh rose geranium, for garnish (optional)

Petite strawberries, for garnish (optional)

My daughter absolutely loves this shake. It takes the classic strawberry milkshake to a whole new level. One of my ideal treats is sipping on this delectable milkshake with a homemade cheeseburger or veggie burger and rose-salted French fries. (Yes, taste it! It's the best.) It's over-the-top and totally delicious. I highly recommend the indulgence.

MAKES 4 SMALL OR 2 LARGE MILKSHAKES

Add the ice cream, milk, and Rose Geranium and Strawberry Jam to a blender and blend on high speed until the mixture is well combined, about 30 seconds. Evenly divide the milkshake between four medium or two large tumblers. Serve immediately with a straw and garnish with a rose geranium bloom and a petite strawberry, if desired.

ROSY CHOCOLATE MALTED MILKSHAKES

12 oz [340 g] chocolate ice cream

⅓ cup [80 ml] whole milk

3 Tbsp malted milk

¼ tsp rose water

Fresh roses, for garnish

A beloved nostalgic treat is given a dose of elegance with a touch of aromatic rose water. If you love the sweet flavor of rose, this indulgent dessert is for you. Garnish with a petite fresh rose and surprise your loved one with an unexpected sweet.

MAKES 4 SMALL OR 2 LARGE MILKSHAKES

Add the ice cream, whole milk, malted milk, and rose water to a blender and blend on high speed until the mixture is well combined. You may need to use a rubber spatula to scrape down the sides if the mixture isn't combining easily.

Pour the milkshakes into four medium or two large tumblers. Garnish with roses and serve immediately with a straw and a spoon.

BLOOMING ROCKY ROAD ICE CREAM

ICE CREAM BASE

2 cups [480 ml] half-and-half

3 Tbsp high-quality maple syrup

¼ cup [20 g] Dutch-processed cocoa powder

5 large egg yolks

1 cup [240 ml] whole milk

½ cup [100 g] granulated sugar

¼ tsp Rose Salt (page 15)

ROSE-SALTED ALMONDS

⅓ cup [50 g] raw almonds

¼ tsp Rose Salt (page 15)

1 cup [40 g] Hibiscus Marshmallows (page 133) or plain marshmallows, cut into ½ to ¾ in [12 mm to 2 cm] cubes

½ cup [90 g] chopped 70% dark chocolate

Chocolate ice cream with homemade Hibiscus Marshmallows (page 133), toasted Rose-Salted Almonds, and dark chocolate?! Yes, this fancy-pants ice cream is over-the-top and absolutely heavenly. Serve in a sugar cone and top with an additional Hibiscus Marshmallow and Rose-Salted Almond for the prettiest ice cream cone you've ever seen.

SERVES 6

To make the ice cream base: In a Dutch oven set over medium heat, vigorously whisk together the half-and-half, 1 Tbsp of the maple syrup, and the cocoa powder to incorporate the cocoa. Once it's well mixed and steaming, remove the Dutch oven from the heat. Pour the mixture into a large heatproof bowl, place a fine-mesh sieve over the bowl, and set aside.

Place the egg yolks in a medium heatproof bowl and set aside.

Return the Dutch oven back to medium heat. Add the milk, sugar, remaining 2 Tbsp of maple syrup, and the Rose Salt and stir constantly. Once the mixture begins to simmer, ladle about one-quarter of the mixture into the bowl with the egg yolks and whisk until combined. Pour the egg yolk mixture back into the Dutch oven and continue to stir constantly with a wooden spoon, making sure the mixture doesn't

CONTINUED

get too hot or boil, lowering the heat as needed. Once the mixture begins to thicken and coats the back of the wooden spoon (about 5 to 7 minutes), remove the Dutch oven from the heat and pour the mixture through the fine-mesh sieve resting over the bowl with the cocoa powder mixture. Cover the bowl and place it in the refrigerator for at least 1 hour to cool. You can speed up the process by placing it in the freezer for 30 minutes.

To make the Rose-Salted Almonds: While the base cools, place the almond in a small cast-iron skillet over medium heat. Sprinkle with the Rose Salt and toast for 5 to 10 minutes, shaking the pan to flip the almonds every minute or so. Remove the pan from the heat and allow the almonds to cool completely. Once cool, set a few almonds aside for garnishing, then chop the remaining almonds and set aside.

To make the ice cream: Take the ice cream mixture out of the refrigerator, pour it into an ice cream machine, and churn the mixture according to the manufacturer's instructions. When the ice cream is ready, use a rubber spatula to fold in the Hibiscus Marshmallows, chopped Rose-Salted Almonds, and chocolate. Transfer the ice cream to a large glass storage container, cover, and place in the freezer for at least 1 hour before serving.

Scoop the ice cream into your favorite ice cream cone. Top with an additional Hibiscus Marshmallow and Rose-Salted Almond, if desired. This ice cream keeps in an airtight container in the freezer for up to 2 weeks.

HIBISCUS MARSHMALLOWS

¾ cup [180 ml] cold filtered water

1¼ oz [35 g] unflavored gelatin

1 cup [200 g] granulated sugar

⅓ cup [105 g] organic light corn syrup

2 Tbsp dried hibiscus, ground

1¼ tsp Rose Salt (page 15)

1 tsp coconut oil, melted and cooled, for greasing the pan and knife

¼ to ½ cup [25 to 50 g] sifted confectioners' sugar, for coating the pan and topping the marshmallows

These prettiest-of-pink marshmallows make a glamorous topping to hot chocolate, are perfect for roasting in the most gorgeous of s'mores (see page 134), and of course are wonderful when added to Blooming Rocky Road Ice Cream (page 131).

MAKES APPROXIMATELY
20 LARGE MARSHMALLOWS

Pour ½ cup [120 ml] of the water into the bowl of a stand mixer fitted with the whisk attachment. Pour the gelatin powder over the cold water and let sit for about 10 minutes.

Meanwhile, in a medium saucepan over medium heat, bring the granulated sugar, corn syrup, hibiscus, ¼ tsp of the Rose Salt, and the remaining ¼ cup [60 ml] of water to a boil, using a wooden spoon to stir the mixture until the sugar has dissolved. Attach a candy thermometer to the side of the pan and bring the mixture up to 240°F [116°C], stirring occasionally.

When the sugar mixture comes up to temperature, return to the stand mixer and beat the gelatin mixture on low speed. Very slowly and carefully, stream the hot sugar mixture into the bowl of the stand mixer. Gradually increase the speed of the mixer until you've added all of the hot sugar mixture. Beat on high speed for several minutes until a thick, fluffy, pink marshmallow batter has formed, 8 to 10 minutes.

CONTINUED

You will have extra marshmallows if you make a batch to add to the Blooming Rocky Road Ice Cream (page 131), so bring the extras on your next camping trip to make the prettiest s'mores you've ever had.

Meanwhile, grease an 8 by 8 in [20 by 20 cm] baking pan with the oil and sprinkle liberally with the confectioners' sugar.

Using a clean, slightly damp rubber spatula, spread the marshmallow mixture into the prepared pan. Liberally sprinkle more confectioners' sugar and the remaining 1 tsp of Rose Salt atop the marshmallow. Gently cover and let rest at room temperature for at least 4 hours, or overnight.

Once set, use a spatula to gently remove the whole marshmallow from the pan and place it on a large cutting board heavily sprinkled with confectioners' sugar. Using a sharp knife greased with coconut oil, slice the marshmallow to make about 20 large marshmallows.

Store in the refrigerator in an airtight container for 1 week or in the freezer for up to 1 month.

FLORAL TOFFEE

1 lb [455 g] unsalted butter

2 cups [400 g] packed
light brown sugar

2 tsp lavender, fresh or dried

12 oz [340 g] dark
chocolate (60% cacao)

¼ cup [30 g] walnuts, chopped

½ tsp Rose Salt (page 15)

1 Tbsp dried rose petals

The caramelly smell of fresh, homemade toffee is nostalgia in a nutshell for me. Growing up, every holiday season consisted of my sister and I sneaking into the kitchen to nibble some of my mother's homemade toffee before she handed it out to friends and neighbors. It's a delicious treat . . . sweet, salty, crunchy, and indulgent. With the addition of Rose Salt and crushed lavender, blooms will make their way to the holiday table in stunning fashion.

MAKES APPROXIMATELY
FIFTY 2 TO 3 SQ IN [5 TO
8 SQ CM] PIECES OF TOFFEE

In a medium saucepan over medium heat, add the butter and brown sugar. Attach a candy thermometer to the side of the pan and stir occasionally (keeping a very close eye on it) until the mixture reaches 300°F [150°C].

Immediately (and carefully) pour the mixture onto a standard rimmed baking sheet and sprinkle with the lavender. Break the chocolate into pieces and scatter it on top. Use an offset spatula to spread the chocolate over the toffee until it's completely melted and even, leaving a ⅜ in [1 cm] border of toffee exposed around the outside. Sprinkle the melted chocolate with the walnuts and Rose Salt and place it, uncovered, in the refrigerator overnight.

Remove the toffee from the refrigerator and sprinkle it with the rose petals.

CONTINUED

Break the toffee into pieces with your hands, or transfer it to a cutting board and chop it with a knife, making the pieces as big as you'd like. Store the toffee pieces in an airtight container in the refrigerator (if you keep your home warm and toasty) for up to a week. This toffee can also be stored in the freezer for up to 3 months.

MY FAVORITE EDIBLE FLOWERS: A GLOSSARY, RESOURCE, AND GUIDE FOR USING MY TOP ELEVEN CULINARY BLOOMS

The list of edible flowers is qu[..] extensive. This glossary of som[..] includes my personal favorites [..] have only included blooms tha[..] I have found to be the easiest to source (see page 96) and/ or can be grown organically i[..] your own backyard. The flowe[..] listed below have been include[..] in recipes throughout this boo[..]

CALENDULA

Subtle in flavor, a touch spicy, and vibrant in color, this fresh bloom makes a beautiful garnish in salads and even cocktails. I like to pick off the petals to add to tea sandwiches (see page 86) or to mix in with cream cheese, mascarpone, chèvre, or even butter.

CHAMOMILE

Lovely fresh or dried, this bloom is definitely a favorite of mine. It typically tastes sweet and honey-like. I mostly use the fresh blooms as a garnish and use dried chamomile to make Chamomile Salt (page 14), syrups, and other baked goods. It's fairly easy to source, as you can typically buy organic chamomile tea at your local grocery store and simply open up the tea bags to use the blooms inside. Just be sure to check the ingredient list on the tea you buy since chamomile can sometimes be blended with tea leaves. One of my favorite recipes is my Apricot Chamomile Jam (page 26), which tastes good on just about everything.

PANSY

I only use fresh pansies, and mostly do so to add color to a dish or to use as a garnish. They are perfect to use as a decoration for Floral Doughnuts Four Ways (page 60) or any cakes. I also like to add pansies to ricotta for a burst of color.

HIBISCUS

This dried flower makes an exceptional ingredient. Tart and tangy, it produces an extraordinary color, and I love adding a touch of it to fruit fillings in pies (see page 118), jams, and even yogurt (see page 36). Using dried hibiscus is best, as it's easy to work with and the bloom adds a ton of delicious flavor.

ROSE

I probably use dried and fresh rose petals in my kitchen more than any other edible flower. I grow organic roses at home and use the blooms and petals to garnish many dishes. I love adding fresh rose petals to salads, and dried roses make a delicious Rose Salt (page 15), which I add to pretty much everything these days for both flavor and aesthetics. Depending on the type of rose you source, the flavor can be sweet, fragrant, and even a bit tangy. I always encourage tasting while cooking with blooms so you can get a sense of what the flower tastes like rather than blindly following a recipe. One dried rose can differ from the next to such an extreme degree, so it's important to taste what you buy before you cook with it. My Rose Petal French Toast (page 43) is the ultimate ode to the edible flower I most adore.

CONTINUED

BORAGE

Borage has the most beautiful color. I love using this bloom as a garnish or in floral ice cubes. It makes a beautiful topper for cupcakes (see page 107) and is also lovely to use in floral butters and cream cheese tea sandwiches (see page 88). The flavor is quite subtle with just a hint of citrus and warm spices.

NASTURTIUM

Where I live, nasturtiums grow wild everywhere and all year round. We always have many nasturtium blooms in our garden, so it's fun to have fresh blooms to pick and nibble on throughout the year. I have experimented with using nasturtiums in syrups and baked goods and have found that their flavor is best when freshly picked and not cooked. They are spicy and colorful, and each color tastes just a little different. I adore mixing the petals into my favorite salads, floral butters, ricotta, and even mascarpone or cream cheese for a beautiful floral garnish (see page 88).

LAVENDER

The flavor of lavender is lemony and vibrant. I have found that dried lavender can taste more potent than fresh, so taste it before you cook with it to assess its richness. A jar of dried lavender looks so beautiful on the kitchen counter and lasts for as long as a few months. Add it to meat marinades, classic cocktails, butter, and sugar (see page 19). One of my favorite cocktail recipes in my book *Floral Libations* is the Lavender Gin Daisy, which is made with lavender-infused gin—a must-have when entertaining guests. My Lavender Butter (page 20) is delicious on top of homemade crepes or melted into your favorite morning toast.

ROSE GERANIUM

This beauty has the most incredible fragrance. Use the leaves in syrups (see page 22), jams (see page 23), ice creams (see page 124), and cocktails (see page 93). The blooms are also lovely to use as a garnish for your favorite dishes. My Rose Geranium Ice Cream (page 124) is a beautiful way to celebrate this wonderfully fragrant plant.

HERB BLOOMS

Rosemary, thyme, chives, sage, basil, arugula . . . so many herbs, when left to bolt, will produce the most beautiful blooms. Sprinkle herb flowers on toasts, sandwiches, eggs, and even in yogurt. They each have a different flavor profile, and experimenting with herb flowers is a fun way to see a different side of your favorite herb. Place a variety of blooms on an assembled cheese board to delight guests with their beauty and aroma (see page 74). Or use them to season a homemade quiche (see page 66) or even a favorite libation.

LILAC

The fragrance and color of these magnificent, fleeting blooms are absolutely glorious. I get so excited when our lilacs start to bloom that I start making a list of recipes I want to remake or try out as soon as I see the little purple flowers start to open up. I mostly like using lilacs fresh, though they make an amazing simple syrup (find the recipe in my book *Floral Libations*). Use lilacs as a garnish, make lilac sugar, or sprinkle them atop your favorite breakfast dish (such as the Blueberry Lilac Dutch Baby on page 53). These blooms are beautiful, pleasantly fragrant, and taste like spring.

FLORAL RECIPES FOR DIFFERENT OCCASIONS

▨▨▨▨▨▨▨▨▨▨▨▨

MOTHER'S DAY BRUNCH:

Rose Petal French Toast with Rose Butter and Rose Geranium Syrup (page 43)

Champagne with a Rose-Salted Rim (page 95)

Calendula Sourdough Waffles with Nasturtium Butter and Floral Infused Honey (page 45)

Strawberry Chamomile Doughnuts (page 64)

Lavender Crepes with Lavender Pluot Sauce (page 37)

ROMANTIC EVENING AT HOME:

A Floral Cheese Board (page 74)

Rose Geranium Gin Daisy Cocktail (page 93)

Jasmine Flourless Chocolate Cake (page 109)

Berries with Lavender Whipped Cream (page 79)

KID'S BIRTHDAY PARTY:

Strawberry and Rose Geranium Milkshakes (page 127)

Chocolate Cupcakes with Rose Buttercream Frosting (page 107)

Boysenberry Jasmine Doughnuts (page 65)

BRIDAL SHOWER:

Garden Party Layer Cake with Strawberry Hibiscus Jam Frosting (page 111)

Floral Toasts Four Ways (page 82)

Strawberry Shortcake with Chamomile Whipped Cream (page 102)

Rose Geranium Gin Daisy Cocktail (page 93)

A Floral Cheese Board (page 74)

BABY SHOWER BRUNCH:

Jasmine Sticky Buns (page 59)

Floral Doughnuts Four Ways with Hibiscus Lemon Glaze and Fresh Edible Flowers (page 60)

Plum Lavender Clafoutis (page 56)

Homemade Chamomile Granola and Hibiscus Parfaits (page 34)

Coffee with Garden Party Creamer (page 69)

Calendula, Gouda, and Bacon Quiche with Fresh Blooming Herbs (page 66)

HOUSEWARMING PARTY:

Olallieberry Hibiscus Pie (page 118)

Rose Geranium Ice Cream (page 124)

Garden Party Stone Fruit Galette (page 115)

Floral Chèvre and Chamomile-Salted Cucumber Tea Sandwiches (page 86)

AFTERNOON TEA:

Watermelon Radish, Spring Pea, and Borage Cream Cheese Tea Sandwiches (page 88)

Raspberry Elderflower Scones (page 90)

Berries with Lavender Whipped Cream (page 79)

Orange Blossom and Chamomile Chocolate Pumpkin Bread (page 80)

Apricot Chamomile Jam with Ricotta and Chopped Pistachios on Toast (page 83)

Rose Geranium Gin Daisy Cocktail (page 93)

HOLIDAY TEA PARTY:

Floral Toffee (page 135)

Chocolate Cupcakes with Rose Buttercream Frosting (page 107)

Champagne with a Rose-Salted Rim (page 95)

A Floral Cheese Board (page 74)

Orange Blossom Chocolate Hazelnut with Rose Petals on Toast (page 28)

Ebleskiver with Rose Confectioners' Sugar (page 50)

GIRLS' NIGHT IN:

Rosy Chocolate Malted Milkshakes (page 128)

Chocolate Chip Cookies with Rose Salt (page 101)

Almond Butter with Chamomile Salt and Floral Infused Honey on Toast (page 82)

Rocky Road Ice Cream (page 131)

FAMILY GAME NIGHT:

Lemon and Hibiscus Ice Pops (page 122)

Strawberry and Rose Geranium Milkshakes (page 127)

Chocolate Chip Cookies with Rose Salt (page 101)

Rosy Rosemary Chamomile-Salted Roasted Cashews (page 77)

BIRTHDAY BREAKFAST IN BED:

Garden Party Pancakes with Lavender Syrup (page 48)

Jasmine Sticky Buns (page 59)

Rose Petal French Toast with Rose Butter and Rose
Geranium Syrup (page 43)

Calendula, Gouda, and Bacon Quiche with Fresh
Blooming Herbs (page 66)

Coffee with Garden Party Creamer (page 69)

Blueberry Lilac Dutch Baby (page 53)

AUTHOR BIO

Cassie Winslow is the founder of the blog *Deco Tartelette* and the author of *Floral Libations*. Her work has been featured in *O, The Oprah Magazine*, the *New York Times*, *Vogue Paris*, *Forbes*, *Grub Street*, and *Brides Magazine*. She lives in Santa Cruz, California, with her husband, daughter, and rescue pup, where they tend to their delightful edible flower gardens.

Photo by: Nicholas Winslow

ACKNOWLEDGMENTS

To Nicholas, your love and unwavering support is what fuels me to do it all.

To Charlotte, your passion and vibrancy puts a skip in my step and inspires me daily.

To Morgan, for encouraging me to pursue my creative aspirations amidst the engagements of our own adventure.

To Deanne, my editor—since day one, it has been such a treat to work with you. I am beyond grateful.

And to my mother, thank you for your unfaltering support and for giving me permission to share our family recipes with a floral twist.

INDEX